CHILDREN OF ISRAEL

The Story of Temple Israel

MEMPHIS, TENNESSEE: 1854-2004

BY JUDY G. RINGEL

TEMPLE ISRAEL BOOKS

Combustion
Temple Israel Books
Memphis, Tennessee
ISBN 0-9759436-0-X

Printed in the U.S.A.

The publication of *Children of Israel*
was underwritten by a grant from the
L'Dor Vador Fund at Temple Israel,
and by an anonymous benefactor.
Proceeds will be used to benefit the
Temple Israel Archives.

To Bradley, Joel, Brian,
Erin, and Matthew, who represent the next
generation of Temple Israel

Acknowledgements

Almost from the start, the leaders of Temple Israel kept wonderfully detailed records. Had they not done so, I could not have written this book. The minutes of the congregation, begun in 1857, include not only the nuts and bolts of Temple Israel's history — committees appointed, votes taken, resolutions adopted — but also the particulars of thousands of discussions on everything from ritual changes to building and maintenance concerns. A vivid portrait of the congregation at each stage in its history, the minutes were the source of most of the details in this book; likewise, they were the source of all quotes not otherwise attributed.

Happily, the work of collecting, organizing, and preserving the congregation's historical documents is an ongoing project, thanks to Shirley Feibelman, who had the foresight to establish the Temple Israel Archives in 1987, and to her daughter-in-law, Linde Feibelman, who currently oversees the Archives. I am especially grateful to Linde and to Margery Kerstein, who were the tour guides for my two-year journey through Temple's vast store of archival material. Their participation in this project was, in a word, indispensable.

The importance of Marcia Levy's participation also cannot be overstated. Serving as copy editor and research assistant, she corrected my punctuation, helped check facts, and tracked down missing information with the determination of Sherlock Holmes. Her keen eye and attention to detail were a tremendous help.

A number of other people also provided valuable assistance: Hallie Elliot and Martha Graber generously undertook the time-consuming task of sifting through the Archives' enormous collection of photographs. Betsy Saslawsky skillfully organized marketing and special events for the book, with help from Susan Lindy, Hallie and Russ Elliot, Melissa Faber, and Jimmy and Janice Ringel. In the Temple office, Carol Geller and Zane Kay graciously put up with my frequent interruptions, Bonnie Cooper took the time to look through hundreds of snapshots, and Lucy Beck responded promptly and cheerfully every time I called — which was often — to ascertain the correct spelling of a former member's name or to double-check some other vital statistic.

I was fortunate to have two earlier chronicles of Temple Israel's history at my disposal: the first was written by Babette M. Becker in 1929 on the occasion of the Temple's seventy-fifth birthday; the second, titled *Our First Century*, was written in 1954 by Helen G. and Rabbi James A. Wax, and edited by Ernest Lee, in conjunction with the congregation's centennial celebration. Selma S. Lewis's history of the Memphis Jewish community, *A Biblical People in the Bible Belt*, also provided a wealth of information, as did John E. Harkins' history of Memphis and Shelby County, *Metropolis of the American Nile.*

My deep appreciation goes to everyone who took the time to read the manuscript: writers Sanford Jacobs, Perre Magness, and Jonathan Ringel; book publisher Rollin Riggs; Rabbis Harry Danziger and Micah Greenstein; former Sisterhood President Jocelyn Rudner; and every member of my immediate family, including my mother, Ernestine Greenberger, who first inspired my love of the written word, and my sister, Ruth Lester. The feedback I received from these discerning readers was extremely helpful.

If it's true, as the saying goes, that a picture is worth a thousand words, then I owe at least fifty nods of appreciation to Billy Riley and Combustion, whose gorgeous design for the book and its cover turned my fifty-thousand-word manuscript into a work of art. Collaborating with Billy was a special privilege; his devotion to this project went way beyond the call of duty. I was also privileged to work with photographer Murray Riss, whose interior and exterior shots of the Temple building, which appear in these pages, vividly portray the Temple's architectural beauty.

During the two and a half years that I worked on *Children of Israel*, Rabbi Micah Greenstein and former President Kenneth Wurzburg were a huge source of strength. For their unbridled enthusiasm for this project — which never wavered, even though I made them wait until I had finished writing the entire book before allowing them to read a single page — I owe them both a huge debt of gratitude.

Finally, I would like to say a heartfelt thank-you to my husband, Nick, who encouraged me to embark on this journey and cheered me on, every step of the way. His love and support are, quite simply, the bedrock of my life.

J.G.R.
JUNE 2004

Preface

In her introduction to the book *Profiles of Courage for Our Time*, Caroline Kennedy tells of a visit she once made to the Senate Reception Room in the U.S. Capitol, accompanied by her uncle, Senator Ted Kennedy, and her daughter, Rose. As the three of them stood there and gazed up at the portraits of legendary former senators, Ms. Kennedy writes that she "felt a continuity of spirit reaching across time and into the future . . . ."

Her words struck a familiar chord with me. Looking back through a century and a half of Temple Israel's history, I too felt "a continuity of spirit reaching across time," the shared commitment to Judaism that tied each rabbi, and each group of officers and trustees, to all those who preceded them and all who would come afterward. Indeed, while the history of Temple Israel could be told in terms of the three fine houses of worship it has erected, or in the number of Torahs and Jewish artifacts it has accumulated, the real story lies in the determination of the Jewish pioneers who formed the congregation back when Memphis was just a rowdy frontier river town, and in the dedication of the men and women who sustained it, through good times and bad, for 150 years.

Thousands of individuals have contributed their time, talent, and financial resources to Temple Israel over the past fifteen decades, and many more have congregated, worshipped, and studied in its midst. Unfortunately, not all their names — or their deeds — are recorded in the annals of the congregation; nor, regrettably, are they all included in this book. Nevertheless, this project has given me a deep appreciation for the generations of lay leaders and volunteers who made Temple Israel a priority in their lives. It is largely through the work of their hands that the congregation has remained vibrant and strong.

And so this book is dedicated to every member, known or unknown, who ever served on a committee, planned a program, taught in the religious school, sang in the choir, wrestled with the budget, chaperoned a youth group, prepared a congregational meal (or cleaned up after one), ushered at services, worked in the library, directed traffic, helped with a mailing, called on the sick or bereaved, raised needed funds, donated needed funds, or participated in the myriad other activities that have nourished this congregation for 150 years.

It was 1854, seven years before the start of the Civil War, and Memphis, Tennessee, was a boomtown on the edge of the western frontier.

Just thirty-five years after it was founded as a cluster of log cabins perched on the Fourth Chickasaw Bluff — hence the nickname "Bluff City" — the tiny settlement had blossomed into a lively center of trade and commerce.

Picture, if you will, what Memphis was like back in the mid-1850s, before the streets were paved, before the bridges over the Mississippi were built, and long before such conveniences as automobiles and electric lights (and air conditioning!) were invented. The best way to reach Memphis, or leave it, in those days was by steamboat on the mighty Mississippi, since travel and communications by land were rudimentary, at best. Still, progress was underway. In 1854 the city's first railroad, the Memphis & Charleston line, extended only about forty-five miles east to LaGrange, Tennessee; by 1857 the track was completed, with much fanfare, all the way to the East Coast. A year later, in September 1858, even the West Coast came into reach for those willing to risk the journey, when stage coaches began carrying passengers and mail from Memphis to California.

Barring Indian attacks, the trip could be accomplished in 34 days.[1]

Within the city limits, an area that covered three square miles, signs of progress were everywhere. Cotton was the backbone of the local economy, and the effort to supply growers' needs and provide a market for their crop had spawned a galaxy of new businesses: warehouses, brokerage firms, and all manner of wholesalers and retailers, including a number of slave traders. The Farmers and Merchants Bank, the city's oldest

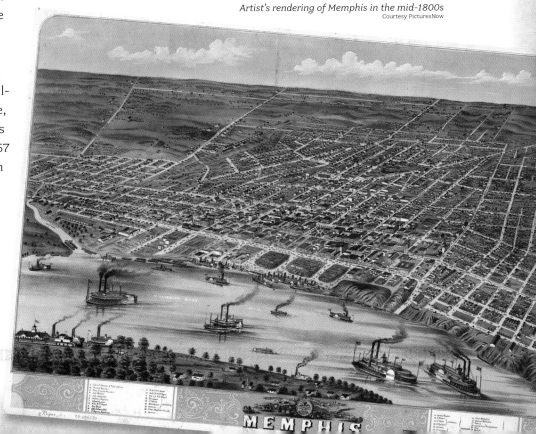

Artist's rendering of Memphis in the mid-1800s
Courtesy PicturesNow

MEMPHIS

financial institution, found itself with two new competitors during the 1840s; by 1860 the Farmers and Merchants was defunct, but as many as twenty other banks had opened for business.[2] A daily newspaper, *The Appeal,* was established in 1841 and was soon joined by a handful of other publications. While Memphis could hardly be described as urban during the last decade before the Civil War — stray cattle, after all, still wandered into Court Square — by the end of the 1850s it had acquired most of the basics of a real city: brick buildings on Main Street, a board of health, a volunteer fire department, a couple of policemen/night watchmen, free public schools.[3] It even had a few frills: an upscale hotel known as the Gayoso House, a Thespian society, and improbably, a historical society called Old Folks of Shelby.[4] In addition, it had more than a few churches: groups of Methodists, Catholics, Episcopalians, Presbyterians, and Baptists had already erected houses of worship.[5]

This, then, was the Memphis that attracted thousands of new settlers to the bluffs of the Mississippi River during the 1840s and '50s. The local population, which numbered just 1,799 in 1840, ballooned to 8,841 by 1850, due in part to the city's merger with the community of South Memphis, which had developed south of Union Avenue. By 1860 the number of residents more than doubled again, to 22,623. At this point in its history, Memphis was growing more rapidly than any other city in the nation.[6]

While most of the newcomers were Southerners who drifted west from Virginia and the Carolinas, a sizeable percentage — nearly one-fourth — were foreign immigrants, primarily from Ireland and Germany. Among the Germans, there was a sprinkling of Jews. And among the Jews was a man named Joseph I. Andrews.

Joseph Andrews was not the first Jew known to have lived in Memphis. That distinction apparently belongs to David Hart, who came to Memphis from Germany in 1838, operated Hart's Inn and Saloon on Adams Street between Front and Main, and moved away sometime during the 1850s or '60s.[7] Joseph Andrews, however, was the first to begin planting Jewish roots.

Andrews, whose mother, Sallie Salomon Andrews, was the daughter of Revolutionary War supporter Haym Salomon, arrived in Memphis in 1840 from Charleston, South Carolina.[8] He became a successful businessman, with interests in cotton, banking, and brokerage enterprises, and built the city's first three-story home, at the corner of Court and North Second.[9] It says a great deal about Andrews — and about Memphis — that just seven years after his arrival, this Jewish newcomer was sufficiently prominent to serve as one of the city's ten aldermen for the years 1847-48.[10]

When his brother, Samuel, died in 1846, Andrews bought a parcel of land on Bass Avenue (later Jefferson) to be used as a Jewish cemetery. The event was pivotal for the small group of Jews living in Memphis, in that it marked the moment when they began to function as a Jewish community. Four years later, in 1850, they formed a Hebrew Benevolent Society to oversee the cemetery and dispense charity, as needed. And three years after that, they set about organizing the city's first synagogue.

No one knows exactly when the Jews of Memphis began holding religious services, but it is likely they were worshipping in private homes during 1853, and especially likely that they gathered to observe the High Holy Days in the fall of that year. Officially, Temple Israel came into being on March 2, 1854, when the Tennessee Legislature granted a charter of incorporation to The Congregation of the Children of Israel (also known as B'nai Israel) "for the purpose of establishing in the city of Memphis a church for the worship of Almighty God according to the rites and creed of the Hebrew sect." Though the congregation actually numbered thirty-six families at the outset, the charter lists ten men — a *minyan**— as the original incorporators: J.I. Andrews, Moses Simons, John Walker, D. Levy, Julius Sandac, T. Folz, M. Bamberger, M. Bloom, Jos. Strauss, and H. Reinach.

Early on, the young congregation received a much-needed windfall: a $2,000 bequest from the estate of philanthropist Judah Touro of New Orleans. They used

JUDAH TOURO

The New Orleans philanthropist helped finance the new Jewish congregation in Memphis.

the money to buy a lot on Second Street, but eventually sold it again, probably because they lacked the necessary funds to build on it. For the first few years they held "divine services," as they called them, in a number of different places. Then, late in 1857, they leased the old Farmers and Merchants Bank Building at the corner of Main and Exchange and set about remodeling it for use as a synagogue, with seating for 150 men and 50 women.

It was an ambitious project for the fledgling congregation, and Joseph Strauss, who served as president in 1857-58, had to call a number of special meetings to work out the details. Should they build a separate gallery for ladies in the new synagogue? The members said yes, by a vote of eighteen to fourteen. How should they finance the remodeling costs? Two separate committees were appointed, one to solicit contributions from "all the Israelites in this city," the other, surprisingly, "to receive subscriptions from Gentiles." As was customary at the time, they raised additional money by selling members their seats in the new building. At an auction on March 18, 1858, fifty "gents" seats were sold for a total of $343, and forty-four ladies' seats, for $158.

While the congregation was Orthodox at this point in its history, it is an indication of the direction in which the majority of members were leaning that they invited Dr. Isaac Mayer Wise, the founder of American Reform Judaism, to come to Memphis to dedicate the new synagogue. Wise accepted, and on March 26, 1858, the dedication ceremony took place. (During the same visit, Wise helped to form Lodge No. 35 of B'nai B'rith, the forerunner of the Sam Schloss Lodge.) Two days later, the congregation adopted a flowery resolution in Wise's honor, expressing the hope that "the seeds planted by him on our fruitful Southern Soil may be productive of that Piety he so energetically seeks to spread over the length and breadth of this land."

Thus the synagogue was launched. In the beginning, the entire congregation — that is, all the men in the congregation — met quarterly, or more often, if necessary, to discuss whatever matters were pending. Attendance at meetings was mandatory; members who skipped a meeting

ISAAC MAYER WISE

The founder of American Reform Judaism dedicated Children of Israel's first synagogue.

*A glossary of Hebrew terms can be found on page 131.

without an acceptable excuse — as, for example, Edward Barinds, Moses Levy, R.L. Lasky, and Isaac H. Lehman did on October 25, 1857 — were fined fifty cents apiece.

Conscious of their vulnerability as a small religious minority in a very Southern, very Christian environment — a fact of life that would continue to influence the congregation's attitudes and actions throughout its history — the members instituted a number of practices that were designed to safeguard their image in the community. For starters, they did not automatically roll out the welcome mat for every Jew who wanted to join. Applications for membership were approved or disapproved by secret ballot, and members were permitted to blackball candidates they deemed unworthy of admission. It took five blackballs for an applicant to be rejected. The congregation also adopted a process whereby it could suspend or expel from its ranks any member who acted "in a disreputable manner so as to bring discredit upon his character and thereby injure the good standing of the congregation."

Despite these measures, members' behavior at early meetings often reflected the rough-and-tumble frontier culture that prevailed in Memphis at the time. One night in December 1857, a meeting of the congregation was disrupted by what is referred to in the minutes as certain "difficulties that occurred between Messrs. H. Caro and M. Bloom." While Caro and Bloom apparently buried the hatchet a few days later, the members decided to amend the bylaws to try to prevent the eruption of similar "difficulties" in the future. "Whereas, owing to disturbances that have so frequently disgraced our meetings," they wrote, "and in consideration that we as a society do not wish to be considered as living in a community where might is considered as right, Be it therefore resolved that

1) Any member of this congregation who uses abusive or threatening language towards either officers or members shall be fined ten dollars, and 2) Any member . . . who shall cause a fight or disturbance during a meeting *or who shall bring with him concealed weapons of any description* shall be fined not less than ten dollars or more than twenty-five dollars."[11]

Lacking a rabbi during the first few years, the congregation relied on part-time cantors to lead its worship services. Jonas Levy was the first of these, followed by H. Judah and J. Sternheimer. By April 1858, however, the members had accumulated enough money to pay a full-time spiritual leader, so they placed advertisements in the *Israelite,* a newspaper published in Cincinnati by Isaac Mayer Wise, and other Anglo-Jewish papers for "a Lecturer, Reader and Teacher to lecture in English and German, and to lead a choir, at a salary of $600 a year, with perquisites to add $400 more." At the same time, they also advertised for a *shochet* — that is, a kosher slaughterer — who would be paid $300 per year, "independent of poultry killing." On the recommendation of Rabbi Isaac Leeser of Philadelphia, the foremost Orthodox spiritual leader in America at that time, the congregation voted on December 6, 1858, to hire the Rev. Jacob J. Peres to serve as "*Chazan* and Teacher" — in essence, to be its first rabbi.

Born and educated in Holland, Jacob Peres was a prodigy who, by the time he was eighteen, had edited a Hebrew grammar book and a book of proverbs in five languages.[12] After pursuing both secular and rabbinic studies at the Netherlands Israelitish Seminary, he moved to Philadelphia in 1857 and started a school of ancient and modern languages there. He came to Memphis the following year and soon established the city's first Hebrew school.

Under Peres' leadership, Congregation Children of

JACOB J. PERES

Children of Israel's first rabbi, 1858-1860

Israel displayed an amazing sense of *k'lal Yisrael* — a feeling of oneness with all Jews — especially considering the length of time it took in those days for communications to cover the huge distances from one part of the world to another.

At a meeting in January 1860, for example, when congregation Secretary A.E. Frankland read "an account of the suffering Jews in Morocco," one might have expected the members to shake their heads in dismay, murmur a few sympathetic words, and go on to the next item on the agenda. But that is not what happened. First, the members of Children of Israel appointed a committee "to receive donations about the city" for the Moroccan Jews. Then they voted to contribute $50 to the cause from the congregation's treasury, and after that they reached into their own pockets, generously producing an additional $78.75 to help alleviate the distress of fellow Jews in a land that was very, very far away.

With Peres as its spiritual leader, the congregation also continued to adhere to Orthodox tradition, even to the point of adopting a new bylaw to assure that "no person should be called to the Sepher [Torah] on Rosh Hashanah and Yom Kippur [who] violates the Sabbath day." How surprising, then, that just sixteen months after he became the congregation's rabbi, Peres himself was accused by the members of violating the Sabbath.

With a wife and four children to support, Peres was apparently struggling to make ends meet, and he had opened a grocery business with his brother as a way to supplement his income. To the dismay of many members of the congregation, the Peres brothers kept their store open on Saturdays. On April 15, 1860, nearly four months before his contract was up for renewal, the congregation charged Peres with engaging in secular labor on the Sabbath. Three days later they held a formal trial. He was found guilty, and his employment was terminated. Peres later sued the congregation for libel and breach of contract. Though he won the part of the case that involved the salary due him on the remainder of his contract, he lost the libel suit. In a precedent-setting decision, the Tennessee State Supreme Court ruled "that a religious institution is sovereign; that its laws and regulations are supreme;

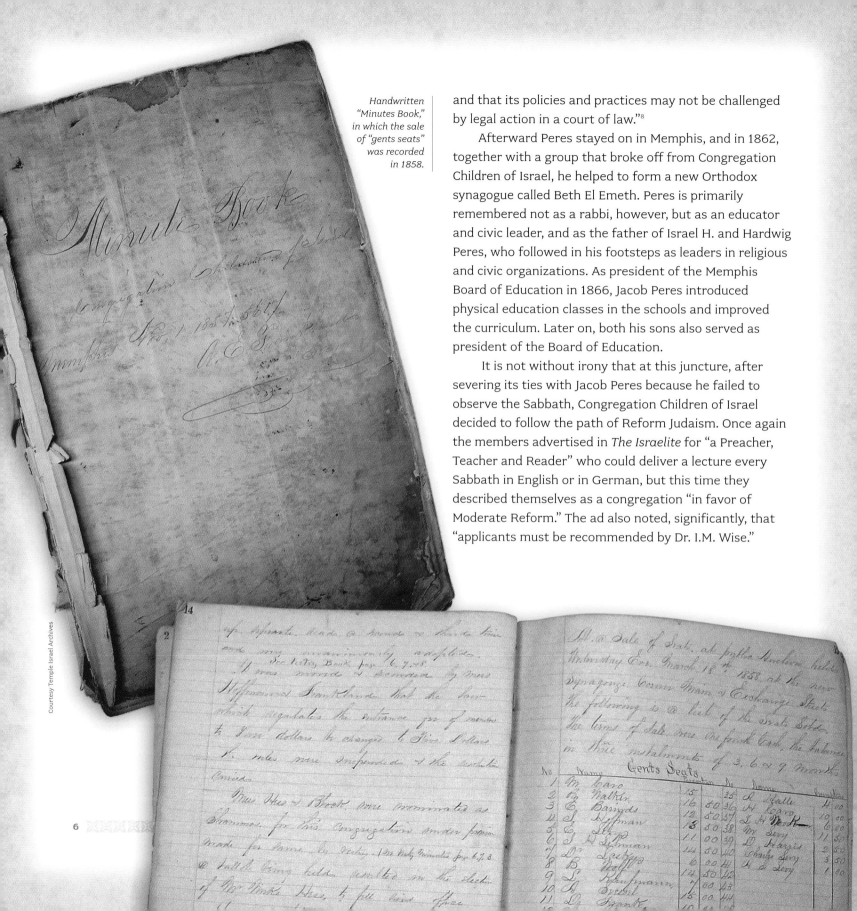

Handwritten "Minutes Book," in which the sale of "gents seats" was recorded in 1858.

and that its policies and practices may not be challenged by legal action in a court of law."[8]

Afterward Peres stayed on in Memphis, and in 1862, together with a group that broke off from Congregation Children of Israel, he helped to form a new Orthodox synagogue called Beth El Emeth. Peres is primarily remembered not as a rabbi, however, but as an educator and civic leader, and as the father of Israel H. and Hardwig Peres, who followed in his footsteps as leaders in religious and civic organizations. As president of the Memphis Board of Education in 1866, Jacob Peres introduced physical education classes in the schools and improved the curriculum. Later on, both his sons also served as president of the Board of Education.

It is not without irony that at this juncture, after severing its ties with Jacob Peres because he failed to observe the Sabbath, Congregation Children of Israel decided to follow the path of Reform Judaism. Once again the members advertised in *The Israelite* for "a Preacher, Teacher and Reader" who could deliver a lecture every Sabbath in English or in German, but this time they described themselves as a congregation "in favor of Moderate Reform." The ad also noted, significantly, that "applicants must be recommended by Dr. I.M. Wise."

Enter Simon Tuska. The son of a rabbi, Tuska was born in Hungary in 1835 and came to America with his family in 1850, settling in Rochester, New York.

Following his graduation from the University of Rochester in 1856, he went to Germany for two years to study at the Breslau Jewish Theological Seminary, where he was the only American student. While in college, Tuska wrote a booklet titled *The Stranger in the Synagogue: The Rites and Ceremonies of the Jewish Worship*, a work he dedicated to Thomas J. Conant, a Christian clergyman.[19] He also wrote a number of articles for *The Israelite*, which may have been what brought him to the attention of its editor and publisher, Isaac Mayer Wise.

Wise recommended Tuska for the rabbinical position in Memphis, and on July 1, 1860, the congregation elected him unanimously over three other candidates:

SIMON TUSKA
Spiritual Leader of Children of Israel, 1860-1870

Cohen of St. Joseph, Deinwater of Chicago, and Saiser of Rochester. He was hired initially for three years, at a salary of $800 a year.

If the congregation wanted a reformer, they certainly found one in the twenty-five-year-old Tuska. Starting in August 1861, when he suggested that nearly all the *piyyuttem,* or poems, be eliminated from the service, Tuska guided the congregation toward a modification of traditional Orthodox ritual, deleting components of the service he believed were antiquated and adding features he felt were more relevant to life in nineteenth-century America. In November 1862, with Tuska's blessing, the congregation voted to organize a choir, for which a committee was appointed to solicit not just men, but "ladies and gentlemen of the Jewish faith from the ages of nine years and upward." Under the direction of the cantor, Mr. Ritterman, the newly formed choir of four men and ten women began participating in services in the spring of 1863, just in time to enhance the splendor of another innovation that Tuska introduced in May of that year — a ceremony called Confirmation.

At three o'clock on the afternoon of Shavuot in 1863, a standing-room-only crowd gathered to witness the first Confirmation class enter the synagogue in procession: three girls clad in white dresses with blue sashes, and four boys dressed alike in suits adorned with blue rosettes, each child carrying a bouquet of flowers that was deposited, ever so carefully, on the lectern. The congregation was "affected to tears at the blessing of the children," one member later wrote of the occasion. During the two-hour ceremony, the member added, Tuska "held his audience spellbound . . . explaining to them in a beautiful sermon that a public confirmation of children was not a matter to be so dreaded by the Orthodox, when they derived an understanding of the principles of our religion from it, had learned the Commandments and knew what was required of them as Israelites, even if they did derive this necessary information from [Isaac Mayer] Wise's *Essence of Judaism*."[15]

More reforms were to follow. In April 1864, at the request of the choir, the congregation permitted an organ to be played during Pesach services. At about the same time, Tuska introduced Wise's abridged prayer book, *Minhag America*. When the need arose for more

Introduced in 1863, the Confirmation ceremony quickly became an annual event. ABOVE, *the Confirmation class of 1872;* RIGHT, *the certificate awarded to Jennie Wolf in 1881.*

CERTIFICATE OF CONFIRMATION

THIS IS TO CERTIFY

seating, the congregation approved a motion to build more pews in both the men's and women's sections — and then, a short time later, they also voted to provide family pews where "ladies and gents" could sit together.

While the members rarely voted unanimously in favor of these reforms, it is clear that most of them heartily approved of Tuska's leadership. In January 1863, six months before his original three-year term of employment was due to expire, the congregation reelected Tuska for ten years, at a salary that would soon reach $1,500 a year. They also passed a resolution heaping praise on Tuska for "having brought order and decorum from chaos and confusion, raised the standard of Judaism to a high point from the dust of indifference, and . . . having spiritually awakened the slumbering energies of his flock even to observe and keep holy the Sabbath day . . . ."

It is noteworthy — and surprising, perhaps — that Tuska's religious reforms were accomplished not during a period of peace and prosperity, but during the turbulent years of the Civil War. Indeed, while Tuska was working to bring order out of chaos within the synagogue, life beyond the synagogue walls was marked by unprecedented disruption and turmoil.

As a trade and transportation hub, Memphis had developed strong commercial ties to both the North and the South before the war, and when talk of secession first began to spread in 1860, most local residents felt their best bet was to stay in the Union. As late as February 1861, the majority of Memphians (and of all Tennesseans) still opposed secession, hoping for a compromise that would save the Union. In April of that year, however, all hope for a compromise between North and South evaporated: Confederate troops fired on Fort Sumter, South Carolina, and in response, President Abraham Lincoln called the Federal troops to arms. Forced to choose sides, Memphians became

ardently secessionist. On June 8, 1861, when a state-wide referendum was held to ratify Tennessee's withdrawal from the Union, Shelby County voted almost unanimously — more than seven thousand in favor, five opposed — to secede.[16]

As far as can be determined, most of the members of Congregation Children of Israel agreed with — or at least went along with — the secessionist fervor that swept the city. Whether they were motivated by deep personal conviction or whether their views simply echoed the prevailing attitude of their neighbors, the congregation embraced the Confederate cause with apparent enthusiasm. Even the rabbi was heard beating the drums for war. "The Jews of Memphis are ready, in common with their Christian brethren, to sacrifice their property and their lives in defense of Southern rights," Tuska proclaimed when hostilities broke out, thereby resolving any doubt that might have existed in the community about whether the Jews would be loyal to the Confederacy.[17]

Tuska probably received little or no direction from his rabbinical colleagues on the critical issues of slavery and secession. With few exceptions, rabbis on both sides of the Mason-Dixon Line, as well as the Jewish press, avoided sermonizing on these divisive subjects before the war started, no doubt in the belief that American Jews in 1860 were too few in number, too vulnerable, and in historian Selma Lewis's words, "too newly arrived" to have their leaders go out on a political limb.[18]

Even Isaac Mayer Wise and Isaac Leeser, the two most prominent American rabbis of the day, adamantly refused to speak out on the issues that were tearing the country apart. Wise went so far as to publish an editorial titled, "Silence, Our Policy." According to the noted American Jewish historian, Rabbi Jacob Rader Marcus, Wise viewed the threat to the Union as the greatest calamity facing the nation. He believed, at least in the beginning, that the Union had to be preserved at all costs — even at the cost of tolerating slavery. In a time before social justice became the clarion call of Reform Judaism, "this truly great man," Marcus wrote, "betrayed no understanding of the moral issues involved in slavery."[19]

Be that as it may, by 1861 the war was on, and the residents of Memphis, Jews and Gentiles alike, soon became caught up in it. Memphians rejoiced when word came in July 1861 of the Confederate victory at Manassas (Bull Run); in their excitement, the city's aldermen promptly named a street in honor of the battle. And on a Saturday morning shortly afterward, Congregation Children of Israel gave a proud and patriotic send-off to more than ten of its own men who had

The Great Naval Battle At Memphis by Alexander Simplot, 1881

enlisted in the Confederate Army. The volunteers, "all uniformed in Confederate gray, marched into the building during Sabbath services," congregation President A.E. Frankland, a staunch supporter of the Confederacy, later wrote in his memoirs. "Standing round the scrolls of the law, they recited the blessing, in chorus: Major Abraham S. Levy, Captain Maurice A. Freeman, Lieutenant Isaac Strauss, Corporal M.A. Kuhn, Privates Lou Leubrie, Samuel Jackson, Harry Cohen, Julius

Hoisting the Stars and Stripes Over The Post Office by Alexander Simplot, 1862

Nathan, Emil Gross, Harry Jessel, and several others. After this they received the priestly benediction from the minister and returned to the camps of their several commands. It was their last assemblage together, and was a sad realistic scene that will never be forgotten by those that witnessed same."[20]

More sadness was soon to come. By the summer of 1862, just a year after the war started, the Confederate Army had surrendered Nashville, lost the bloody battle at Shiloh, and abandoned Fort Pillow, the last Southern stronghold upriver from Memphis. Now the city was open to attack from both the north and the east. At dawn on June 6, while thousands of area residents watched from the safety of the bluffs, what was left of the Confederate River Defense Fleet confronted the Union's ironclads as they steamed southward on the Mississippi River. It was not much of a contest. In less than ninety minutes, the Union won. Later that day, a detail of Union soldiers hoisted the

Stars and Stripes above the post office, and from that time on until the war ended nearly three years later, Memphis was occupied by Federal troops.

While the city suffered little or no physical damage from the Civil War, its spirits were certainly dampened by the combined humiliations of defeat and occupation, food and clothing shortages, rampant inflation, casualty lists that grew ever longer as the war dragged on, and finally, Reconstruction. Still, the residents of Memphis proved amazingly resilient. Within a year after it fell to the Union, the city was, quite literally, back in business. "Memphis is the metropolis of the Southwest," Jacob C. Cohen, a Jewish officer from New York who was stationed near Memphis, wrote in a letter to *The* [New York] *Jewish Messenger* on June 2, 1863. "Traders have flocked here from New York, St. Louis, Louisville, and Cincinnati. And at all hours of the day, the streets present a busy appearance." Which was not to say the streets presented a cheerful appearance. "I have no doubt but that there are five of the gentler sex in Memphis to each male," Cohen continued, "and what makes this fact more apparent is *that at least one-third are in mourning* — probably for lost relatives in the war."[21]

Cohen, whose unit of the Ohio Brigade earlier had camped in and around Corinth, Mississippi, was delighted when they moved closer to Memphis in June 1863, since it gave him the opportunity to visit what he called the "Main Street Congregation" — that is, Congregation Children of Israel — where he noticed "several blue coats [Union soldiers] among the worshippers." In what later generations of Jews would refer to as a "small Jewish world experience," he recognized the cantor, Mr. Ritterman, as none other than the former cantor of the Greene Street Synagogue in New York. Cohen was surprised to find such a well-organized Jewish community so far out in the boondocks. "The Jewish population here is considerably larger than I anticipated," he wrote to *The Messenger*. "It is estimated that there are at least a thousand of our co-religionists here at present; they manage to support two synagogues, three charitable societies, two clubs, besides a literary society, & etc."[22]

Cohen's estimate of the Jewish population was too high; according to the 1860 census, only about four hundred Jews were living in Memphis. He noted correctly, however, that they were well established in the community. Following the pattern of Jewish immigrants all over the South, most of the men had started out as peddlers, but within a few years they had parlayed the profits from their pushcarts into small retail or wholesale businesses. D. Bloch was among the first to set up shop; he opened a men's furnishing store as early as 1850. Other early arrivals included D. Levy, who had launched a retail clothing business by 1855; Benedict Lowenstein, who opened his first small dry goods store at Poplar and Front Streets in 1855 and made enough money to bring his brothers, Elias, Abraham, and Bernard, over from Germany to help in the endeavor; Henry Seessel, who in 1857 established a butchering business that his descendants would build into the Seessel's supermarket chain (later Schnuck's); and Solomon Halle and his brothers, who established the men's clothing store, Oak Hall, in 1859.

By 1863 there were Jewish merchants in Memphis selling just about every commodity people wanted to buy, including liquor (D. Hirsch; Nathan, Judah and Co.; E. Mayer and Co.; H. and L. Morgenthau; E. and L. Block); tobacco (D. Kauffman and I. Samelson); crockery (A.S. Milius); jewelry (Joseph Goodman); patterns (M.L. Putzel); hats (Jacob Bloch); shoes (Strauss, Lehman, and Company and Zellner Shoe Company); and dry goods (Menken and Brothers; Loeb and Holland; Lazard Kremer). Theobald Folz was operating a boarding house, A.E. Frankland was an auctioneer, and a few men, including A. Genzburger, S. Isaacs, and L. Helman, were in the cotton business.[23] So prominent were the Jews on the commercial scene, in fact, that on the day after Yom Kippur in September 1863, the Memphis *Daily Bulletin* reported that "the large Jewish element of Memphis was made manifest yesterday by the number of closed stores on Main Street."[24]

Also prospering in Memphis at the time were scores of speculators who had swarmed into the city like locusts after Memphis surrendered to the Union. Aided by members of the Union Army, these civilian profiteers seized the opportunity to make huge commissions by trading cotton, which was in short supply in the North, in exchange for gold and silver, quinine (to treat malaria), surgical supplies, and arms, all of which were desperately needed by the South. In spite of being occupied by Federal troops, Memphis quickly became a center of illegal trade and a conduit through

Bales of cotton lined up for shipment on the Memphis cobblestones.

operations of certain non-Jews from coming to light. And still others claim that Grant himself was deeply and unapologetically anti-Semitic. Whatever the case, on December 17, 1862, Grant's headquarters in Holly Springs, Mississippi, issued what is perhaps the most extensive anti-Jewish regulation in the nation's history — General Orders, No. 11, which began as follows: "The Jews, as a class violating every regulation of trade established by the Treasury Department and also department orders, are hereby expelled from the department [of Tennessee] within twenty-four hours from the receipt of this order."[26]

Cesar Kaskel, a Jewish resident of Paducah, Kentucky, and clearly a man of action, immediately fired off a sixteen-line telegram to President Abraham Lincoln protesting Grant's order. When he failed to receive a reply (there is no evidence that Lincoln ever saw the telegram), Kaskel hopped on a boat to Cincinnati to confer with Isaac Mayer Wise and line up support for the Jewish cause. From there he went to Washington, D.C., where Ohio Congressman John Addison Gurley, a friend of Wise's, arranged for Kaskel to meet face-to-face with Lincoln. The meeting went well. After learning of Grant's unconstitutional eviction order, Lincoln reportedly summed up the situation by asking, "And so the children of Israel were driven from the happy land of Canaan?" Kaskel answered him in kind: "Yes, and that is why we have come unto Father Abraham's bosom asking protection." To which Lincoln is said to have replied, "And this protection they shall have at once."[27]

which thousands of dollars worth of contraband supplies were being funneled to the Confederacy.

To say that the Union Army's top brass was frustrated by the situation would be an understatement. Generals William T. Sherman and Ulysses S. Grant were infuriated, and they were determined to put a stop to the illegal trading. Still, their first efforts in this regard were inconsistent and ineffective. Upon taking over command of Memphis in November 1862, General Stephen A. Hurlbut complained that "bribery and corruption" had seeped into every branch of service.[25]

What happened next has been the subject of much commentary. Some historians say it was Hurlbut who first blamed the Jews for the problem of illegal trading. Others suggest the charge was made by officers on Grant's staff who were hoping to keep the smuggling

Lincoln wrote a note to General-in-Chief of the Army Henry W. Halleck, instructing him to telegraph Grant to cancel the eviction order. Kaskel carried the note to Halleck, along with a copy of Grant's infamous order, and on January 4, 1863, Halleck dutifully sent the following wire to Grant: "A paper purporting to be General Orders, No. 11, issued by you December 17, has been presented here. By its terms, it expels all Jews from your department. If such an order has been issued, it will be immediately revoked." Three days

GENERAL-IN-CHIEF HENRY W. HALLECK

later Grant revoked the order, making sure to indicate the recall was not the result of any second thoughts on his part, but was issued "by Direction of General-in-Chief of the Army, at Washington." In other words, he was just following orders. Halleck, too, made it clear he was just following orders. In a letter to Grant dated January 21, 1863, Halleck explained that it was not he, but the President, who had "deemed it necessary to revoke" the order, "as it . . . proscribed an entire religious class, some of whom are fighting in our ranks." [28]

Jewish soldiers were, indeed, fighting in the ranks of the Union Army, and General Orders, No. 11, did nothing to enhance their respect for Ulysses S. Grant. In a letter to *The Jewish Messenger* from Corinth, Mississippi, on May 6, 1863, Jacob Cohen left no doubt about his bitterness toward his commanding general. "It seems to be pretty clearly demonstrated," Cohen wrote, "that the Army of Tennessee wants a *leader*; that is, a man who . . . can refrain from kicking Israelites out of his back door, while the enemy enter at the front; a man who is a man, and a General; one who is free from the bigoted principles which are demoralizing our army and rendering our success more uncertain and distant."[29]

While the Jews of Memphis were no doubt stunned and shaken by the blatant discrimination inherent in Grant's order, they were not directly affected by it; during the brief time the order was in effect, no forced evacuations were carried out in Memphis. The city's Jews *were* affected, however, by an order that was issued by the Union Army on November 20, 1863, which required all merchants "not having permission from these Headquarters to keep and sell military clothing" to ship their stocks of merchandise north of the lines of the department of Tennessee. The order named fifteen stores that had stocks of military clothing on hand without the proper authority. All fifteen were owned by Jews. As historian Bertram Wallace Korn noted in *American Jewry and the Civil War*, "Unless one finds it logical that fifteen Jewish merchants could be guilty of illegal practices, while two non-Jewish competitors were not, the only conclusion is . . . prejudice was the controlling factor."[30]

Somehow the Jews of Memphis managed to endure these anti-Semitic incidents — a testament to their fortitude, if nothing else — but they never forgot who stirred up all the trouble, and who it was who came to their aid. When Abraham Lincoln was assassinated on April 14, 1865, Congregation Children of Israel joined with Beth El Emeth to hold a memorial service for the slain president, and Sam Schloss led a contingent of B'nai B'rith marchers in the city's official mourning parade. Three years later, when Ulysses S. Grant ran for president, the Jews of Memphis came together once again — this time to adopt a resolution branding Grant as "a man unfit for the high position to which he aspires, and incapable of administering the laws to all classes with impartiality and without prejudice."[31] Leaders of the Jewish community urged Memphis's Jews to use "every honorable means" to defeat Grant, and they encouraged Jewish communities in other cities to do likewise, although as far as is known, Nashville's Jews were the only ones who followed suit.[32] It is interesting to note that Grant's campaign in 1868 marked the only time, before or afterward, that the Memphis Jewish community ever took a united stand in a presidential election.

Artist's rendering of Abraham Lincoln's funeral procession in Washington, D.C., April 1865.

Ultimately, the Jews of Memphis made it through the 1860s by doing whatever they had to do to weather the hard times. When wartime conditions resulted in the closing of several schools, Congregation Children of Israel took on the responsibility of operating a day school "for all branches" — Christian as well as Jewish. Organized by Lazard Kremer, William Milius, and S. Myers, the Hebrew Educational Institute opened its doors at 109 Madison Street in August 1864, with a principal, Andrew J. Haile, and four teachers: Rabbi Tuska (languages), Sigmund Schlessinger (music, German, and Hebrew), Mrs. Annie Haile (instructor in the Female Department), and Miss Annie Coolidge (teacher in the Primary Department). At least a hundred students attended the Hebrew Educational Institute during its first term, but despite its success, the school lasted for only a few years. Lacking the funds to keep it going, the congregation voted to close it down in 1868.

Nor was the Hebrew Educational Institute the only project that Congregation Children of Israel had trouble funding in the aftermath of the war. Expenses regularly exceeded income during the period, a situation that led the congregation to raise its dues in 1867 to $4 a month per member. (Increases to $7 and $8 a month were considered, but voted down.) A year later, when it became apparent that the increased dues income was not going to cover the shortfall, a motion was adopted, after much discussion, to assess each member according to his means.

Back in 1860 the congregation had arranged to buy the synagogue building it was leasing at Main and Exchange, and by November 1864, despite the economic disruptions caused by the war, the members had managed to pay off the mortgage. Thus by the end of the war the building was a ready source of needed cash. In 1867, facing yet another budget deficit, the congregation voted to take out a $5,000 mortgage. Three years later, nineteen members, including Elias Lowenstein, Henry Seessel, D. Menken, B. Eiseman, E. Ackerman, and M. Friedman, lent the congregation a total of $1,000, interest free, so that the mortgage could be reduced. Rabbi Tuska offered to add $250 to that amount out of his own pocket, but the congregation declined his offer.

Meanwhile, Congregation Children of Israel continued to move, gradually but steadily, toward Reform Judaism. During the war Tuska introduced a Thanksgiving service and a National Fast Day service, both of which, while suitably patriotic for the times, were unheard of in traditional Jewish ritual. Then, at a special meeting on January 22, 1870, the congregation took a giant step away from Orthodoxy. By a vote of twenty-eight to four, the members changed the starting time of the Friday evening "divine service" from just after sunset — which in December meant that Sabbath prayers would begin in the late afternoon — to 7:30 p.m., a time that was much more convenient for men who were, for the most part, making their living as shopkeepers. A few years later they moved the High Holy Day services to 7:30 p.m. as well. At the same time, the members began to let go of their German past. When Tuska asked for instructions on how to lecture during the Friday evening services, he was requested, according to the minutes of the meeting, "to do it in the English language."

There is no way to know where Tuska's leadership might have taken the congregation in the years that followed, because he died of a heart attack in December 1870, at the age of thirty-six. Still, one thing is certain: the eleven years Tuska spent in Memphis were pivotal for Congregation Children of Israel. Amid all the disruptions of the Civil War and Reconstruction, this innovative rabbi showed his congregation a way to modernize and Americanize the traditional rituals of their ancient faith, and he guided them as they took their first bold steps along that path. By the time of Tuska's death in 1870, Congregation Children of Israel had made the transition from Orthodox to Reform.

Wanted: "A minister and Reader, at a salary of $2500, who can preach in English and in German."

Congregation Children of Israel consisted of about a hundred members in February 1871 when it advertised in *The Israelite* and *The* [New York] *Jewish Times* for a new spiritual leader. This time as many as ten rabbis applied for the position — a measure of the growing size and strength of the American

MAX SAMFIELD
Spiritual Leader of Children of Israel, 1871-1915

Jewish community — and on June 18, 1871, the members gathered at the synagogue on Main Street to make their selection. President Elias Lowenstein gaveled the meeting to order and led the members through a careful review of the candidates' qualifications. Not until all of the other applicants had been considered did Lowenstein bring up the name of Rev. Max Samfield, reminding the members that Samfield was "the young minister who, on his way from Cincinnati to his present home in Shreveport, Louisiana, stopped in our city and preached an approbation lecture on last Sabbath."

The young minister's Sabbath lecture must have been quite an impressive one, for when the matter was finally put to a vote, he received forty-one of the forty-eight ballots cast. Samfield was elected to serve as the rabbi of Children of Israel for a period of one year. He would stay for nearly half a century.

Like his predecessor, Samfield was a European immigrant and the son of a rabbi. Born in Marksteft, Bavaria, in 1844, he completed both secular and rabbinic studies at three institutions of higher learning in Germany before coming to America in 1867. His first rabbinical position in the United States was with B'nai Zion Congregation in Shreveport. On August 18, 1871, at the age of twenty-seven, he was installed as the spiritual leader of Congregation Children of Israel in Memphis.

"Brethren of the Congregation B'nai Israel, I am now yours," Samfield boldly declared in his inaugural sermon from the pulpit of the little synagogue at Main and Exchange. "The vigor of my youth, the faculties of my soul, the energies of my mind; nay, my very life, I consecrate to your moral welfare and to the welfare of Judaism and humanity." Accompanied on the pulpit by four of the congregation's lay leaders — Lowenstein, Herman Gronauer, Adolph Loeb, and Henry Seessel — the new rabbi, a short, studious-looking man with a benevolent smile, spoke to the members from his heart and instantly captured theirs when he concluded with these words: "I will share your joys and sorrows; your children shall be my children. Let us be a band of brothers who, without contention, strive to secure peace as the greatest blessing here on earth and eternal salvation as their reward in the world beyond."[33]

Though no one knew it at the time, Samfield's words that day were prophetic. In the coming years, the young rabbi would indeed find it necessary to devote his faculties and his faith — even at the risk of his life — to the welfare of the congregation and the general community. And he would be called upon, all too often, to share his congregation's sorrows.

Yellow fever, a viral infection spread by a mosquito called *Aedes aegyptus*, had plagued various parts of the country, especially New Orleans and the lower Mississippi Valley, since before the Revolutionary War. Memphis itself had already suffered two outbreaks of the disease: the first, in 1855, resulted in 220 deaths; the second, in 1867, killed 595.[34] But even this second outbreak did not serve as the wake-up call the city desperately needed. In spite of repeated warnings by the Board of Health, which had been

urging city officials for more than a decade to install a sewage system and implement other sanitation measures, Memphis remained during the 1870s a virtual cesspool, a city where garbage was thrown into the streets and raw sewage was dumped into rivers and bayous. While it is true that Memphis was in dire financial straits in the wake of the Civil War and Reconstruction, it was not just a shortage of funds that caused the city's aldermen to ignore the danger of epidemic; it was also their defeatist attitude toward the problem. The connection between hygiene and disease — and between stagnant, polluted water and mosquitoes — was only beginning to be understood in those days, and many of the city's government and business leaders still held the belief that there was little or nothing they could do to ward off an epidemic.[35]

Thus Memphis was ripe for catastrophe. It struck in the summer of 1873, when the city took a triple-hit from cholera, smallpox, and yellow fever. Of these, yellow fever wreaked the most havoc: over five thousand cases were recorded, and more than two thousand deaths.[36] And that was not the worst of it. Five years later, in July 1878, yellow fever broke out again in the city. By August of that year, when the Board of Health finally admitted at least one person had already died from the disease, Memphis was in the throes of a full-blown epidemic, and its residents were in a state of panic. In less than a week, more than twenty thousand people fled the city. Traveling by whatever means possible, they went wherever possible — many of the Jews went to St. Louis — until the outlying towns, in an effort to protect their own citizens, imposed a quarantine to keep the Memphians out. With no place else to go, an estimated five thousand refugees from Memphis set up a makeshift camp a few miles outside the city.

Virtually overnight the city's pre-epidemic population of more than 40,000 was cut in half. Of the estimated

A.E. FRANKLAND

The congregation's president during the 1860s and its warden in the 1870s, Frankland wrote an account of the 1873 yellow fever epidemic for B'nai B'rith.

20,000 citizens who stayed, nearly 85 percent are thought to have contracted yellow fever, and 5,150 people died. And even that was not the end of it. The following summer, yellow fever struck again. Though the epidemic of 1879 was less severe than the earlier outbreaks, an estimated 2,000 people came down with the awful disease that year, and more than 550 died.[37]

The grim details of the Jewish community's losses are contained in the annual reports compiled by the congregation's former president, A.E. Frankland, a meticulous record-keeper whose duty it was, as warden of Children of Israel during the 1870s, to supervise the operations of the cemetery. Frankland, who also served as "Grand Nasi" of B'nai B'rith Lodge No. 7 and president of the Hebrew Hospital Relief Association, wrote a separate report of the 1873 epidemic for B'nai B'rith. At the height of the fever outbreak, the local B'nai B'rith chapter had organized volunteer nurses, and the national organization had sent in monetary aid.

During the seven weeks between September 14 and November 5 of 1873, Frankland recorded 51 burials in Children of Israel's cemetery — nearly twice as many as the cemetery normally handled

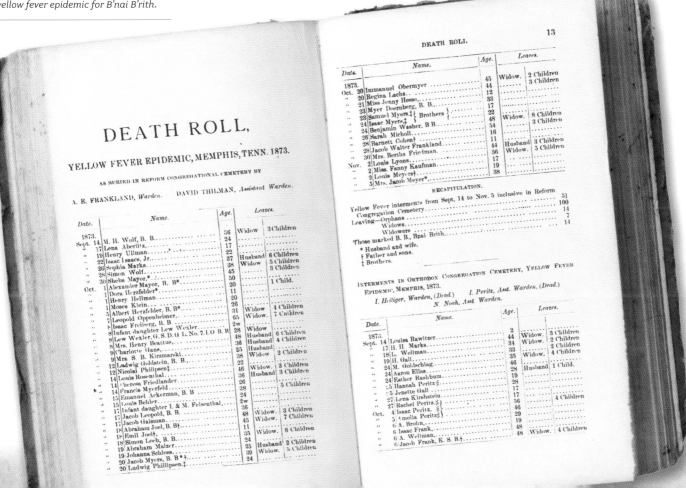

in an entire year — and 43 burials in what he called the "Orthodox Congregation Cemetery," the one owned by Beth El Emeth. The toll on individuals and families from that single epidemic was devastating: 31 women in the Jewish community lost their husbands, 11 men lost their wives, 158 children lost one parent, 23 children lost both parents, and 17 families buried a child.[38]

Among the members of Children of Israel who perished during the 1873 epidemic was twenty-eight year-old Lew Wexler, the congregation's enthusiastic former secretary, whose wife of eleven months had just given birth to the couple's first child. A few hours before Wexler died, his two-week-old daughter also died. Also on the list of victims were Samuel Myers, age thirty-three, and his brother Isaac, seventeen, who died within hours of each other; Simon Loeb, thirty-five, who left a wife and six children; Mrs. Henry Beatus, forty-eight, who left a husband and six children; and A.E. Frankland's own son, Jacob Walter Frankland, age eleven.[29]

Five years later, when the fever struck again, there were 78 burials in Children of Israel's cemetery. This time the victims included Theobald Folz, an original incorporator of the congregation, who had served as its sexton for many years. The following summer, yet another man associated with the congregation's early years succumbed to yellow fever — Jacob Peres, its first rabbi.

Among those who stayed in the city throughout all three of the fever outbreaks was Rabbi Max Samfield. All during the long, hot months when the disease ran rampant, when business ground to a halt and all types of communal gatherings were prohibited — even, at times, religious services — Samfield worked alongside other members of the clergy to ease the suffering of the city's residents. "Amidst this carnival of death, our unassuming Rabbi moved as a hero," the congregation recalled in a resolution adopted many years later in Samfield's honor. "Throughout the long days he labored. Throughout the long nights he watched. No call upon his services [was] unheeded; no demand upon his time ignored. He ministered to the sick; brought consolation to the stricken; gave sympathy to the orphan; and by the torch light, buried his dead. In his services for good, he made no distinction, either in race or condition, but the Gentile as well as the Jew were the beneficiaries of his volunteer services."

Other members of Congregation Children of Israel also chose to stay and help, many at great sacrifice. As a volunteer with B'nai B'rith, Benjamin Washer helped organize and dispatch nurses in 1873 and died in the process. In the aftermath of Washer's death, Henry Seessel "jumped into the breech," A.E. Frankland wrote. "After burying his own sister, two nephews, and one niece, he reported again to us for duty, visited the sick, supplied nurses and stood firm by us to the last." Seessel was one of a dozen men, according to Frankland, "who never, under any circumstances, missed a funeral, in the capacity of pallbearers."

His cohorts in this so-called "Corporal's Guard" included Emanuel Levy, Jonathan Rice, Ellis Leubrie, Lou Leubrie, Samuel Dreyfus, Dave Eiseman, G.H. Judah, N. Noah, J. Sartorius, and A. Rosenstiel.[40]

When yellow fever broke out again in 1878, congregation member Nathan D. Menken sent his wife away from Memphis, but at the last minute, in response to an urgent call for volunteers by an organization of caregivers known as The Howards, he decided to stay in town to help nurse the sick. Like so many others, Menken, too, died of yellow fever.[41]

In addition to the staggering death toll, the epidemics also exacerbated Memphis's financial troubles. Saddled for years with an unmanageable debt, the city now had no hope of digging itself out; its population had fallen by half, and most of those who remained did not have enough money to pay their property taxes. Memphis was bankrupt. In January 1879 the state of Tennessee revoked the city's charter, took over the management of its affairs (including the appointment of city officials), and reduced its status to that of a "taxing district," an ignoble distinction Memphis would carry for the next fourteen years. Among the first reforms implemented by the Memphis Taxing District were strict new sanitary regulations. With these new measures in place, the city at long last cleaned up the mosquito-infested areas and effectively put an end to the devastating epidemics.

Though the 1870s could hardly be characterized as a period of prosperity, a few members of the congregation actually launched new businesses during the decade — notably brothers Jacob and Isaac Goldsmith, who opened a little dry goods store in 1870 that would eventually grow into the city's largest department store chain, and A. Schwab, whose sundry store on Beale Street, founded in 1876, would still be doing business in the same location

more than 125 years later. But in the wake of the disastrous epidemics, most local organizations, for-profit as well as not-for-profit, were struggling to stay afloat. Congregation Children of Israel was no exception. "The late epidemic . . . left the financial condition of our congregation, like everything else, unsettled," congregation Secretary Samuel Hirsch reported when the membership was finally permitted to assemble for its annual meeting in November 1878, after the fever outbreak had subsided. With $1,600 in unpaid dues, the congregation was unable to pay $750 owed to Rabbi Samfield in back salary and an equal amount owed to Elias Lowenstein, who had paid some of the congregation's expenses out of his own pocket. In a surprising display of optimism, given the circumstances, Hirsch suggested that an influx of fifteen or twenty new members, "[who] I think can easily be induced to join us," would help put the congregation's balance sheet back in the black. The Finance Committee, comprised of H. Bensdorf, B. Eiseman, and Isaac Schwab, came up with its own plan to erase the deficit: each member should "make a small sacrifice" and purchase his seat in the sanctuary.

However they managed it, just as the city itself found the means to recover from the devastation, so too did Congregation Children of Israel. In the case of the congregation, the rebound was remarkably swift. By September 1880 the membership had increased to 124 families, and at the annual meeting, then-President G.H. Judah predicted that within a year, the congregation would be out of debt entirely. "It is gratifying indeed and should be a pleasure to us all," Judah proudly declared, "that with all the trials and troubles of past years, our congregation has not diminished in membership, and that the spirit of harmony under the guidance of our beloved rabbi has never been excelled at any time during the existence of

TEMPLE

OF THE CONGREGATION

"Children of Israel,"

MEMPHIS, TENN.
—RE-TED 1883.—

this congregation." Judah was so optimistic, he expressed the hope that a new house of worship could soon be built.

Children of Israel had bought a lot on Adams Avenue in 1872 with the intention of building on it, but the hardships of the following years had forced the members to put their plans on hold. Now they were anxious to get going on the project. In September 1880 they authorized a committee to dispose of the Adams Avenue property, find a more suitable lot, obtain an estimate of expenses from an architect,

and figure out how to raise the money to erect a new building. It took two years to sell the lot on Adams, but at that point the congregation moved quickly to fulfill its dream. In October 1882 Children of Israel bought a lot on Poplar Avenue, between Second and Third Streets, and proceeded with the design and construction of a new house of worship. As was the case twenty-five years earlier when they

were remodeling the Main Street synagogue, the members kept a close watch on the building process, meeting frequently to resolve construction problems both large and small. At one point a difference of opinion arose over whether the new house of worship should have pews or chairs. Since the members of the Building Committee could not agree on the matter, President G.H. Judah called a special meeting of the entire congregation to settle the question. The vote was unanimous in favor of pews.

The new house of worship was distinctively Byzantine in style, with circular arches above the doorway and windows and twin spires that rose high above its two main towers. Following the trend in the Reform Movement, the congregation called its new building a "temple," rather than a "synagogue." The Poplar Avenue Temple, constructed at a cost of $39,130, was dedicated on January 18, 1884, just six weeks before the congregation's thirtieth birthday.

During its first year in the new Temple, 45 new members joined the congregation, bringing the membership in January 1885 to 173 families. The congregation might have been even larger if the members had accepted a merger proposal made in 1882 by Beth El Emeth, which had been decimated by the yellow fever epidemics and could no longer sustain itself. While Children

PROGRAMME

OF THE

Dedicatory Services

OF THE

Temple "B'nai Israel,"

MEMPHIS, TENN.

Friday, January 18, 1884.

Tracy & Co., print.

of Israel turned the merger offer down — Beth El Emeth had asked that each of its members be given two seats in Children of Israel's sanctuary, free for life — some sort of agreement between the two congregations was eventually reached. Before closing its doors, Beth El Emeth transferred two pieces of property to Children of Israel: a lot next to Calvary Episcopal Church on Second Street that Children of Israel later sold, and Beth El Emeth's cemetery, which Children of Israel held until 1900, when it was purchased by Baron Hirsch Congregation.[42] In the end, however, few if any of Beth El Emeth's members rejoined Congregation Children of Israel, most likely because they were not comfortable with Reform Judaism.

By this time, Children of Israel had been following the Reform Movement for some twenty years, and with Max Samfield as its spiritual guide, the congregation continued to take its cues from Isaac Mayer Wise in Cincinnati. Back in 1873, just two years after Samfield arrived, Children of Israel had joined with twenty-eight other Reform congregations, mostly from the South and Midwest, to form the Union of American Hebrew Congregations. Despite its own difficulties — the summer of 1873 was when the first yellow fever outbreak occurred — Children of Israel had managed to make an initial contribution of $151.50 toward the Union's primary goal of establishing a Jewish theological seminary in America. Two years later, in October 1875, that goal was reached; Hebrew Union College opened in Cincinnati with Isaac Mayer Wise as its first president.

That same month, Rabbi Samfield made a big break with Orthodox tradition in his own congregation when he wrote to the members asking their permission to officiate at services without wearing a hat and gown. In response, the members not only granted the rabbi's request, they went so far as to make it mandatory for *all* the men in the congregation to remove their hats during services. The question of whether or not Samfield should wear a gown, however, was left to the rabbi's discretion. During the following years the members continued to modify their style of worship, often with the intent of making their services — and thus, themselves — appear less foreign. While revising the bylaws in 1881, for example, the members decided that henceforth, they would refer to the *Chazan* as the "Reader."

Meanwhile, there was another matter that required the members' attention. As early as 1875, former President A.E. Frankland and others had begun warning the members that they needed to make arrangements for a new burial ground, because the Bass Avenue cemetery was running out of space. Ten

Courtesy Hebrew Union College–Jewish Institute of Religion

Hebrew Union College, the first rabbinic seminary in America, opened in Cincinnati in 1875.

years later those arrangements finally were made: a ten-acre cotton field on Hernando Road was chosen to be the site of the new cemetery. Children of Israel paid $1,750 for the land, spent another $2,000 on improvements, and dedicated the new burial ground on October 11, 1885. A year later, the congregation spent an additional $1,800 to build a chapel on the property and install some landscaping. (In 1907, the bodies in the Bass Avenue cemetery were disinterred and reburied in a special section of the new cemetery.)

Thus by 1886, less than a decade after the yellow fever epidemics diminished its ranks and tested its staying power, Congregation Children of Israel had managed to regain both its size and strength, its solid financial footing, and its forward momentum. "We estimate . . . to begin this year with . . . about $4,000 net in good assets and no liabilities whatever," the Finance Committee reported at the annual meeting in January 1886. That their balance sheet was in the black was "a splendid showing," the committee

The cemetery chapel remained standing until 1984, when it was deemed unsafe and torn down.

noted, given that the congregation had spent about $45,000 in the previous four years for the new Temple and new cemetery. Indeed, by January 1886 the members of Children of Israel were ready to pat themselves on the back — which is just what the Finance Committee did in the optimistic conclusion to its report: "We heartily congratulate our congregation on the excellent harmony and good feeling prevailing among its officers and members and trust that nothing will transpire to mar the same."

The congregation's recovery did not take place in a vacuum. Starting in 1880 the whole city began to drag itself out of the doldrums, with the result that over the next 30 years . . .

. . . Memphis was virtually reborn as a modern metropolis. So drastic were the changes that Memphis historian John E. Harkins would later write, "A latter-day Rip Van Winkle, going to sleep in 1880 and awakening in 1909, might have thought himself transported to another planet."[43]

To begin with, the 1880s ushered in a period of rapid population growth as thousands of rural migrants, seeking better prospects than they faced as seasonal farm workers, poured into Memphis from the outlying areas of Tennessee, Arkansas, and Mississippi. Between 1880 and 1890 the city's population nearly doubled from 33,592 to 64,495, and by the time of the 1900 census it reached an impressive 102,323, thanks in part to Memphis's timely annexation of twelve square miles of eastern suburbs, an area that contained some 30,000 residents. City officials were so excited about topping the 100,000 mark they declared October 5, 1900, "Census Day" and staged a citywide celebration, complete with speeches and a parade. And who could blame them? According to the census, Memphis had officially surpassed Nashville, Atlanta, and Richmond, Virginia, in population.[44]

Cotton trading still reigned over the local economy, and the heart of its domain was "Cotton Row," the stretch of Front Street between Jefferson and Beale that was lined with brokerage houses and that was

home, since 1873, to the Memphis Cotton Exchange. Now, however, a number of cotton-related industries — ginning, baling, compressing, warehousing — were also developing, and in 1881 local business leaders formed a commodities market, the Memphis Merchants Exchange, to handle cotton by-products such as cottonseed, hulls, and pulp.

Although attempts to broaden the city's economic base beyond cotton were only marginally successful, one area that did develop quickly was the lumber industry. As the virgin hardwood forests around Memphis began to be harvested, lumber quickly

The "Great Bridge at Memphis," also known as the Frisco Bridge, was completed in 1892.

became the city's second most important product.[45] A cluster of related industries, such as barrels, boxes, doors, and wagons, also were developed during this period, as were a number of unrelated industries, including snuff, boots and shoes, and livestock trading.

The addition of seven new railroad lines during the 1880s helped fuel the local economy, but the big boost came in 1892 when the Kansas City, Fort Scott, and Memphis Line built the "Great Bridge at Memphis," the third longest bridge in the world at the time and the only bridge across the Mississippi River south of St. Louis. Four days of festivities in May 1892 led up to the grand opening of the span, which made it possible for thousands of tons of freight to be transported east to west and west to east through Memphis. Ironically, the expansion of the city's railroad system, arguably Memphis's first step in becoming a major distribution center, brought a corresponding decline in shipping on the river. By 1900 steamboat traffic at Memphis had fallen to less than half of what it was in 1880.[46]

Quality-of-life improvements came quickly during the period, starting in 1880-81 when the Taxing District ordered the long-overdue installation of more than thirty miles of underground sanitary sewers. In 1887, an ice company that was doing some exploratory drilling discovered a bonanza just four hundred feet below the city's surface: an aquifer containing billions of gallons of pure artesian water. Soon forty wells were busily pumping clear, clean drinking water, and Memphians were freed, once and for all, from the hazards of consuming contaminated water drawn from their own cisterns or, even worse, from the Wolf River.[47] By 1901 the Board of Health had begun regulating the sale of milk and food and requiring schoolchildren to be vaccinated for smallpox. And at long last the city was regularly picking up the garbage and cleaning the streets. "Like a converted sinner," wrote historian John E. Harkins, "Memphis had achieved a complete reversal on the issues of sanitation and public health."[48] So complete was the reversal that civic boosters, having spent years trying to erase the city's reputation as a place of disease and death, were now promoting Memphis, with some justification, as "the place of good abode."

Abiding in Memphis got even better during this period when two conveniences essential to modern life were introduced: telephones and electricity. With electricity came not just lighting, but improved transportation. By 1900 the Memphis Street Railway Co. was running seventy-five electric streetcars a day in the city over seventeen routes. Automobiles also started showing up on city streets around the turn of the twentieth century, forcing city officials finally to allocate money for street paving, a project that was long overdue.

By any measure, Memphis was growing up. This was the period when the city's first high-rise office building, the eleven-story Continental Bank Building (later named the D.T. Porter Building) was constructed; when the Park Commission was established, and $250,000 in bonds were issued to purchase the two tracts of land that became Overton Park and Riverside Park (later Martin Luther King, Jr.-Riverside Park); when Beale Street was in its heyday, sporting bars, pool halls, pawnshops, and dance halls and spawning the "blues" that became the stuff of legend; and when, for a short time, Memphis even had two horseracing tracks, one of which was touted as the best harness-racing track in the world. (The tracks were doomed in 1905 when the state legislature outlawed pari-mutuel betting.)[49]

To be sure, this was also when the seeds of future problems were sown. It was during this time that Jim Crow laws were enacted to sanction racial separation and discrimination, robbing the city's black residents — 40 percent of the population — of their economic opportunity, to say nothing of their dignity; that funding for public education was relegated to a back burner, a situation that led to the formation of private schools by prosperous white Memphians; and that the city's generally bawdy atmosphere (there were 504 saloons in 1903), coupled with corruption in local government, inspired a reform movement that enabled one man, Edward Hull Crump, to gain political control over Memphis — and keep it — for the next forty-five years.[50]

Still, the ramifications of these events would not be felt for many years. In the meantime, Memphians had their hands full adjusting to the changes that were taking place all around them. For the Jews of Memphis, this meant, among other things, finding a place in their midst for hundreds of Jewish newcomers from Eastern Europe, a small segment of the millions of Jewish immigrants who poured into the United States beginning in

ELIAS LOWENSTEIN
Congregation President, 1870-1875 and 1883-1893

1882, seeking refuge from poverty and pogroms. The city's original German-Jewish settlers — well-educated, financially secure, quite assimilated by now in dress and deportment, and decidedly Reform — had little in common with the impoverished, secularly uneducated, Yiddish-speaking newcomers who bunched together in a neighborhood called the Pinch, just north of downtown. In due course the Eastern Europeans established their own Orthodox congregations: Baron Hirsch, chartered in 1892, which Children of Israel welcomed with the gift of a pulpit and four pulpit chairs; Anshei Sphard in 1898; and two others that were relatively short-lived, Anshei Mischne (1900) and Anshei Galicia (1912).[51]

It was probably enlightened self-interest, rather than pure altruism, that caused the German Jews to help acculturate the greenhorns to America as quickly as possible. They organized a Hebrew Relief Association to provide free loans, sick benefits, and other kinds of assistance to the newcomers, and in the early 1900s they opened a Jewish Neighborhood House in the Pinch, where volunteers provided the new immigrants with health care for their children and free lessons in everything from English to hygiene to civics. Whatever their motives, the ties that bound the German Jews to their Eastern European cousins — and to the religious heritage they shared — were strong: in 1897 the Reform women, working through the Memphis section of the National Council of Jewish Women, organized religious school classes at Children of Israel for the youth of Baron Hirsch.[52] Many of these children continued to attend Sunday school at the Reform congregation until 1907, when Baron Hirsch established a religious school of its own.

As for Children of Israel itself, now that the dramatic events of the 1860s and '70s were fading into history, the membership was finally able to settle down to a period of business as usual. Having weathered the tough times with the rest of the city, the congregation — and especially its rabbi — had earned a place of respect in Memphis, and individual members were increasingly prominent not just on the commercial scene, but also in civic endeavors. Congregation President Elias Lowenstein served on the Board of Health of the Taxing District and was one of ten men selected to help restore the city's charter. When the Tennessee Society for Prevention of Cruelty to Animals and Children was formed in 1880, Rabbi Max Samfield was chosen to be its vice president. And J.S. Menken served on the Memphis School Board in 1895.[53]

By January 1890, Children of Israel's membership

had reached 186 families, and 148 children were attending its religious school — 80 girls and 68 boys, divided into twelve classes and a Confirmation class. "Lessons are given every Sunday morning," President Elias Lowenstein informed the congregation, "in which the branches taught are Biblical History, recital of prayers, Bible reading, Doctrines of Judaism and Jewish ethics, the Festivals and the history of their origins." Fifty-eight girls joined a new juvenile choir, which met twice a month during the winter under the direction of Marie Hitzfield. Within a year, the choir was performing the complete musical liturgy for the Sabbath morning services and was so popular, Lowenstein reported, "it bids fair to become a permanent feature in our Temple service." In every respect, it seems, the Sabbath school was the congregation's shining light. "The discipline maintained is excellent," Samfield wrote to the members of Children of Israel on January 3, 1892, on the occasion of his twentieth anniversary as their rabbi, "and the attendance is far above the average attendance generally attained by Sabbath schools."

So much for the good news. Samfield used the rest of his twentieth anniversary message to reproach the adults of the congregation for their poor attendance at weekly Sabbath services. "The many improvements in our public worship, especially the introduction of prayers in the vernacular and the successful establishment of the Juvenile Choir, have not attracted

as many to the house of God as I had hoped," the rabbi told the members candidly. "The lethargy and indolence of our members," he added, "is still a formidable impediment."

Samfield would continue to sound this sad refrain for a number of years to come, as would the congregation's new president, Herman Gronauer, who was elected in 1894 when Elias Lowenstein finally declined to run again after ten consecutive years at the helm. Gronauer, a deeply religious man who operated an insurance agency in partnership with Samuel Hirsch, the congregation's longtime secretary, approached his presidential responsibilities with a fervor that rivaled the rabbi's. He took office at a time when the nation was in the throes of an economic depression and found the congregation not only financially stagnant, but to his way of thinking, spiritually stale as well.

What Children of Israel needed, Gronauer decided, was new blood — an influx of young men, preferably married, who would revitalize the congregation with energy and purpose and would also help shore up its finances. "The fact must be obvious to everyone that we must awaken the interest of the younger generation in our religion," he told the congregation in 1897, "as we, the old ones, must necessarily leave this field of our activity in the natural course of time, to be replaced by them in their time." To attract these men, Gronauer suggested that the congregation drop its requirement that members buy seats in the Temple's sanctuary. In its place, he proposed the establish-

HERMAN GRONAUER
Congregation President, 1894-1906

ment, on a trial basis, of a category of membership called "seatholder." Seatholders would pay dues — $30 a year for married men, $18 for unmarried men or widows — but they would not have to buy seats. Their seats in the sanctuary would be assigned to them by the Committee on Membership and Rentals, and they would enjoy all the rights of the other members of Children of Israel except the right to hold office.

The A La Mode Club, a group of teenagers whose families were members of Children of Israel, donned military attire for the Purim carnival in March 1898, on the eve of the Spanish-American War. 1) Henry S. Crohn, 2) Leon Benham, 3) Lee Marx, 4) Phil Goodman, 5) Simon Baum, 6) Clarence Coleman, 7) Isse J. Scharff, 8) Sam Nathan, 9) Leon B. Scharff, 10) Fred Goldsmith, 11) Fred Roescher, 12) Albert Hattendorf.

A year later, the seatholder experiment was declared a rousing success. By January 1898, Children of Israel had enrolled 47 new members, and for the first time in four years, the congregation — now 222 families strong — ended its fiscal year with a surplus instead of a deficit. While the turnaround was primarily due to increased revenue, Gronauer also paid tribute to the Finance Committee for having successfully cut expenses. Hardest hit by the budget cuts was the choir, whose annual allocation was slashed from $970.25 to a mere $150. The paid choir, the Finance Committee had noted bluntly, "is not worth the money it costs us."

And so the years passed at Congregation Children of Israel, the changing seasons marked, as in all Jewish congregations, by the solemn observance of Rosh Hashanah and Yom Kippur in the fall and the joyous celebration of Pesach and Shavuot in the spring. Each year brought its own set of challenges and changes. In 1896 Rabbi Samfield introduced the first *Hebrew Union Prayerbook* to his congregation. "In comparison with the old ritual used," President Gronauer observed, summing up the opinion of the members, "it is to be considered an improvement, a change for the better." That same year the congregation made a few alterations in the funeral service in keeping with changes that were being adopted by the Reform Movement, but when a resolution was proposed to drop the requirement that the dead be dressed in a shroud, the members voted — barely — to stick with tradition. Gronauer himself cast the deciding vote on the matter when the congregation became deadlocked, thirty-nine in favor and thirty-nine opposed. He had sought the advice of Isaac Mayer Wise, who believed the shroud should be retained because it symbolizes that all people are equal in death.

The year 1899 brought two exciting announce-ments regarding the Sabbath school: that the congregation had found enough money in the budget to establish a library for the school, and that from now on, instead of having separate classes for boys and girls, all classes would be coed. Samfield, displaying the innocence of the times, said he had adopted the coed plan in the hope "that the lethargy of many a boy will be stimulated to greater interest by the diligence of girls, and that the gentle manners of girls will have a good effect on the discipline of the boys."

In spite of the congregation's progress, however, Rabbi Samfield and President Gronauer continued to be disappointed by the members' poor attendance at Friday night services, and Gronauer, in particular, continued to reprimand them for it. At the annual meeting in January 1899, the president lectured the members on their "chronic indifference to everything that refers to the spiritual side of our congregational life." And a year later, noting with obvious frustration that "even some of the Trustees are absent on Friday eve," he scolded the members again for being "remiss in . . . showing their loyalty to Judaism by their attendance at Divine worship."

It was about this time that the congregation eliminated the position of cantor, opting to rely solely on the choir, accompanied by the organ, for liturgical music. It was also at this time that the question of holding services on Sunday was first considered. Samfield, who did not approve of the idea, nevertheless wanted the issue to be discussed openly. In January 1900 he sent a letter to the entire membership in which he voiced his suspicions that the "empty benches" at Friday evening services were due, at least in part, to a deliberate boycott by members who wanted to move the Friday night services to Sunday morning. "I as rabbi of the congregation have a right to know whether such a hidden cause is in evidence,"

Samfield wrote. He asked the officers of the congregation to bring the question of Sunday services to a vote at the annual meeting. While the congregation did discuss the issue — and while Sunday services were, in fact, adopted by a number of Reform congregations across the country — there is no evidence that a vote on the matter was ever taken by Children of Israel, and the congregation never held Sabbath services on Sunday.

The year 1900 brought news of the death of Rabbi Isaac Mayer Wise, a man "to whom our congregation was especially attached in love and reverence," President Gronauer told the congregation. A memorial service for Wise was held at the Temple on Sunday, April 29, 1900, and for an entire month the Temple building was draped in black.[44]

In contrast, 1901 was a year of celebration for the members of Children of Israel as they recognized the remarkable achievements of their own rabbi, Max Samfield, upon his completion of thirty years as their spiritual leader. In honor of the occasion the congregation resolved to buy or build a parsonage for the rabbi and his wife, Pauline. It took more than a year for them to find just the right property, but in 1903 the congregation bought a two-story brick house at 104 Adams Avenue. The entire remaining balance in the fund that had been established in memory of the yellow fever victims, $4,450, was used to help finance the purchase price of $10,250. Given the courage and dedication Samfield displayed at the time of the epidemics, the trustees of the fund agreed this would be a fitting use for the money.

Congregation Children of Israel celebrated yet another historic occasion in 1905: its "golden jubilee," the fiftieth anniversary of its founding. Exactly why this celebration took place a year late is not known; perhaps someone miscalculated. In any event, the

milestone was marked by an afternoon program of choral music, prayer, and speeches at the Temple, followed by a reception that evening at the hall of the Young Men's Hebrew Association (YMHA), which had been established in 1881.

The honor of delivering the "Jubilee Oration" fell to Rabbi Samfield, but he was far from the only speaker that day. Rabbi Pizer W. Jacobs of Hunstville, Alabama, and the Rev. Dr. Hugh Spencer Williams, pastor of the First Cumberland Presbyterian Church in Memphis, also addressed the congregation, as did Secretary Samuel Hirsch and President Herman Gronauer. When it was Gronauer's turn to take the podium, he looked out at the membership and expressed great pride in their mutual accomplishment. "Fifty years of life, a half-century, have our predecessors and ourselves striven for the preservation of Judaism and for the spiritual progress and material welfare of our congregation," he declared, "and whilst with each year we grow older, we are gaining steadily in energy and strength." Indeed, by the time of its fiftieth birthday, Children of Israel boasted a membership of 262 families, more than seven times the number that had formed the congregation five decades earlier.

Fifty years old and growing, Congregation Children of Israel was not content to rest on its laurels for very long — not with men like Rabbi Samfield and President Gronauer at the helm).

And not as long as the Sabbath school, the rabbi's particular pride and joy, was consigned to cramped quarters in the Temple basement, where the atmosphere was so gloomy, according to Samfield, it bore "the dingy aspect of a dungeon."

Samfield had begun lobbying for improvements to the Sabbath school as far back as 1901, hoping to persuade the congregation to spring for a fresh coat of paint and some new desks, at the very least. Gronauer, too, was convinced of the gravity of the problem, but he had a more comprehensive solution in mind. In January 1906, with more than two hundred children crowded into schoolrooms that were originally designed to accommodate seventy-five, Gronauer gave the congregation, as he had on many previous occasions, his unvarnished opinion of the situation. "The accommodations for our Sabbath school are entirely inadequate," he declared at the annual meeting, "and the Temple itself, built twenty-two years ago, does not meet the requirements of a modern house of worship." Bottom line: the congregation could not ignore the necessity, Gronauer said, of building a new Temple.

Gronauer himself would not live to see the new Temple become a reality. He died at the age of seventy-four in January 1907, just a few days after the congregation's annual meeting that year, the first such meeting since 1894 that he did not chair. Nearly a decade would pass, in fact, before Children of Israel would complete construction of its new facility. Still, it was Gronauer who set the wheels in motion: at the beginning of his last year as president he secured the Board of Trustees' approval to appoint a committee, comprised of Herman Bluthenthal, David Sternberg, Ben Goodman, Sr., H.B. Schloss, and Julius Levy, "to devise the way and means for the erection of a new house of worship and Sabbath school."

Gronauer's successor, Sol Harpman, would not live to see the new Temple either. He was elected president in January 1907, but he died just three months later. Thus it would fall to the two presidents who followed

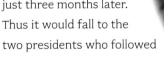

SOL HARPMAN
Congregation President, January-March 1907

Harpman — L.G. Pape and Joseph Newburger — to steer Children of Israel through the perils and pitfalls of yet another building project.

But all that would not take place for several more years. In the meantime, the condition of the Sabbath school in the congregation's existing building demanded immediate attention. Max Sondheimer and Jacob Goldsmith were appointed to head a fundraising campaign, and despite an economic downturn in 1907, a year L.G. Pape later described as one "of unrest, of change, and almost a panic in the business world," they managed to raise enough money not only to enlarge and brighten the school rooms, but also to have fifty-six additional seats installed in the sanctuary.

The extra seating must have been needed only for the High Holy Days, since in 1907 Rabbi Samfield was still complaining about the members' poor attendance at weekly Sabbath services. The members, for their part, were grumbling that the Friday evening services — and in particular, the rabbi's sermons — were too long. The issue had actually come to a head at the annual meeting back in 1898, when, according to the minutes, "Mr. Boshwitz moved that the Rabbi be requested not to hold sermons to last over thirty minutes." Boshwitz's motion failed to pass, though it prompted a lengthy (and, no doubt, very uncomfortable) discussion, but the problem continued to simmer, and it boiled over again at the annual meeting in January 1907. This time it was Samfield himself who turned up the heat. Fed up with preaching to empty pews, he proposed that the trustees of the congregation be *required* to attend services on Friday evenings, and out of respect for the rabbi, the congregation passed a motion to that effect.

Later on in the meeting, after the members had chosen the officers and trustees for the next year, L.G. Pape, the incoming vice president, rose to make a statement on behalf of the congregation. "We the members, assembled at the regular meeting of this congregation, agree to conform with Dr. Samfield's plea to attend divine services on Friday evenings," he declared, "on condition that he limit his lectures to twenty-five minutes and begin the services at 7:30 promptly." Newly-elected President Sol Harpman, who was presiding over his first — and, as it turned out, his last — annual meeting, knew just what to do next. "Meeting adjourned!" he called out quickly, before anything more could be said. The deal was done.

After Harpman's death in March 1907, L.G. Pape assumed the presidency. Like Samfield, Pape had a special enthusiasm for the religious school, and he devoted much of his attention to its operation. During his presidency the congregation began paying a small stipend to the Sabbath school teachers — Pape called the action "a step in the right direction" — and began sending three or four teachers a year to conventions of the Tri-State Sabbath School Teachers Association, which had been organized by Reform Jewish leaders for teachers in Tennessee, Arkansas, and Mississippi.

It was also during Pape's administration that the Ladies' Auxiliary (forerunner of the Sisterhood/Women of Reform Judaism) was formed — which is not to say that Pape was the first president to see the wisdom of inviting the ladies to become more involved in congregational

CONSTITUTION
AND
BY-LAWS
OF

Congregation
Children of Israel

MEMPHIS, TENN.

MAY, 1907

affairs. Herman Gronauer had turned to the women for help back in 1896, when the Temple needed repairs and there was no money in the budget to cover the costs. In response, the ladies put on a fair that lasted an entire week and netted an impressive $3,342.45. In 1898, when $350 was needed for improvements to the cemetery, Gronauer turned to the ladies again, and they came through again, this time by staging a picnic.

Still, nine more years passed before President L.G. Pape issued a call for the formation of an official Ladies' Auxiliary. Eighty-five women, decked out in their best go-to-Temple finery, attended the organization's first meeting. They elected officers — honorary president, Mrs. Dave Levy; president, Mrs. Ben F. Wolff; vice president, Mrs. Sol Coleman; secretary, Mrs. Simon Levi; and treasurer, Mrs. Sam Brooks — and they listened to Pape outline the group's purpose. "The prime object of this society is to aid the congregation in all its endeavors, to serve the cause of Judaism, and especially to promote sociability and friendly intercourse," he told the ladies. Two years later Pape reported the Auxiliary had furnished new covers for the altar, paid for the floor of the Temple to be repainted, and was helping to ensure the attendance of children at Sabbath school. In addition, Pape told the congregation, "The monthly entertainments of the Auxiliary are refined and educated, and by bringing our people together in a social way, they have promoted a feeling of unity. . . ."

By 1910 Children of Israel's membership had grown to 305 families, and Rabbi Samfield, now sixty-six years old, was approaching his fortieth anniversary as the congregation's spiritual leader. In tribute to the rabbi who had guided their path for so many years — the only rabbi most of them had ever known — the congregation elected Samfield "rabbi for life." He would receive a salary of $4,200 a year and retain the use of the parsonage for as long as he lived, and if his wife, Pauline, survived him, she would receive an annuity as well.

At the same time, recognizing the need to relieve the rabbi of some of his duties, the congregation voted to create the position of associate rabbi. Five men were appointed to serve on a search committee — S. Jacobs, B.W. Hirsch, Sam Slager, Joseph Newburger, and Otto Metzger — and in February 1911 they unanimously recommended Rabbi William H. Fineshriber for the position. Since this was the congregation's first experience with having two rabbis in its employ, the members developed a list of rules that defined each rabbi's duties: "1) Sermons shall be delivered in English on Friday nights and Saturday mornings, and the rabbis shall alternate in the delivery of said sermons. 2) The Associate Rabbi shall be the superintendent of the religious school. 3) The Senior Rabbi shall prepare children for Confirmation. 4) Both rabbis shall attend the funerals of members and their families. 5) The rabbi selected by a member of the congregation to officiate at [a] marriage ceremony . . . shall be entitled to the perquisite [gratuity]." Interestingly, the determination of whether an engaged couple was eligible to be married by one of the rabbis was to be made not by the rabbis themselves, but by the congregation's lay leadership. Thus Rule No. 5 continued: "Neither rabbi shall perform said service except upon a written certificate properly signed by the Secretary of the Congregation under the seal of same."

Fineshriber, then thirty-three, was installed as associate rabbi of the congregation in September 1911. A native of St. Louis, he was the first American-born rabbi to serve the congregation, and the first to have been ordained by Hebrew Union College in Cincinnati. Before coming to Memphis, he had worked for ten years — his entire career, up to that point — as the rabbi of Temple Emanuel in Davenport, Iowa.

It was at this point in its history, with 340 families on its membership roster, 260 children enrolled in its religious school, two rabbis to serve its members' spiritual needs, and at long last what President L.G. Pape joyfully characterized as "fine attendance at our Friday eve services," that Congregation Children of Israel turned its attention back to the need for a new Temple. In October 1911, barely a month after Rabbi Fineshriber came on board, Joseph Newburger proposed the formation of a new committee to raise the necessary funds, and over the next year that committee secured $68,000 in pledges. Buoyed by the positive response, the congregation voted in November 1912 to proceed with the construction of a new Temple as soon as possible. The estimated cost, not including the land, was $100,000. Committees were formed immediately. At the outset, Newburger himself headed both the Building Committee and the Finance Committee, but later on Milton S. Binswanger, Sr., was appointed chairman of the Building Committee, with Newburger, Julius Boshwitz, Leon Sternberger, M.H. Rosenthal, Otto Metzger, and David Sternberg serving under him. Sam Schloss headed up the effort to sell the old Temple, and a committee that included C. Haase, Henry Loeb, Frank Kahn, Ben Goodman, Sr., and Jacob Goldsmith took on the task of finding a location for the new one. These men recommended the W.B. Rogers property on the southeast corner of Poplar and Montgomery, and in December 1912, the congregation voted to buy it.

Over the next few years the estimate of construction costs escalated from $100,000 to $125,000, and then to $140,000, and the amount of money the Board was authorized to borrow, originally capped by the congregation at just $10,000, ended up to be four times that amount. Still, the members of Children of Israel stuck with the plan. In 1914 they hired Memphis architects Walk C. Jones and M.H. Furbringer to design the new Temple, and in January 1915 they contracted with the James Alexander Construction Co. to build it.[45] The cornerstone was laid in June of that year.

Meanwhile, the congregation went on with its normal activities, making very few changes in leadership from year to year. L.G. Pape, Sam Schloss, Sam Hirsch, Elias Lowenstein, Joseph Goodman, and other officers and trustees were reelected time and again during this period, retiring from office only when they themselves decided it was time to step down. Lowenstein, for example, served as president of the congregation from 1870-75 and again from 1883-93 — more years, in total, than any other president in the congregation's history. Then he served as warden for ten more years before finally announcing, at the age of seventy-nine, that he absolutely, positively would not run for office again. At that point the congregation elected Lowenstein's business competitor, Jacob Goldsmith, to be the warden, and he held the office for another nineteen years. Remarkably, both Lowenstein and Goldsmith were outdone by Sam Hirsch, who served as the congregation's secretary for more than forty years. When ill health forced Hirsch to step down in 1918,

SAM HIRSCH
Secretary of the congregation for more than forty years

the members recognized his longstanding devotion to Children of Israel by bestowing upon him, along with a number of tangible mementos, the designation "honorary secretary for life."

There was only one person whose extraordinary length of service to Children of Israel surpassed Sam Hirsch's, and that was Max Samfield. By 1915 the beloved rabbi had guided the congregation's spiritual welfare for forty-four years. Along the way he had also found time to serve as a director of the Cleveland Orphans Asylum and the New Orleans Orphan Asylum, both of which had provided a safe haven for Memphis children orphaned by the yellow fever epidemics; as a governor of Hebrew Union College; as a founder of the United Charities of Memphis,

OFFICERS OF THE JEWISH TEMPLE.
AT THE CORNERSTONE LAYING, JUNE 3, 1915.

FRONT ROW (SEATED, LEFT TO RIGHT): *Joseph Newburger, Samuel Schloss, Elias Lowenstein, Sam Hirsch, Samuel Sternberg.* **MIDDLE ROW (SEATED):** *Rabbi Max Samfield, Joseph Levy, B.W. Hirsch, Albert Dreyfus, David Ginsburg.* **MIDDLE ROW (STANDING):** *Simon Jacobs, Rabbi William Fineshriber, Mrs. Hirsch Morris, David Sternberg.* **TOP ROW:** *Elias Gates, Ben Goodman, Sr., Herman Bluthenthal, H. Henochsberg, Sol Isenberg, Leon Sternberger, Otto Metzger, Simon Levi, Joseph Rosenfield. The two children in the photo are unidentified.*

:: Program ::

For the Ceremony of

LAYING OF THE CORNERSTONE

OF

TEMPLE

CONGREGATION

"CHILDREN OF ISRAEL"

Memphis, Tennessee.

THURSDAY, JUNE 3, 1915, 4:30 P.M.

Twenty-third Day of Sivan, 5675.

Master of Ceremonies, Mr. David Sternb

Jos. M. Samfield Printing Co.

the YMHA, and the Hebrew Relief Association; as a volunteer fund-raiser for a number of community organizations, including St. Joseph Hospital; and as the editor and publisher of *The Jewish Spectator*, a weekly journal published in New Orleans and Memphis.

Samfield was already beyond the biblical age of "three score years and ten" when he finally grew weary of his responsibilities; in January 1915 he announced that he wanted to retire, effective October 1. Upon learning of his plans, the congregation elevated Samfield to the status of rabbi emeritus and elected Rabbi Fineshriber, who had served ably as Samfield's assistant for four years, to succeed him.

Sadly, Samfield did not live to enjoy his well-deserved retirement. He died after a short illness on September 28, 1915, just a few days before he was scheduled to step down. In a cruel twist of fate, his funeral was held at the Poplar Avenue Temple on Friday, October 1, the very day he had planned to preach his farewell sermon there and attend a reception in his honor.

The interior of the Poplar Avenue Temple, where Rabbi Samfield's funeral service was held on October 1, 1915. Samfield did not live to see the completion of the new Temple at Poplar and Montgomery.

Inside the Poplar Avenue Temple on the morning of October 1, there was no hint of the festivities that were to have taken place there a few hours later. The crowd that filled the sanctuary was somber, not celebratory. Still, the day turned out, in a strange way, to be just what it was meant to be — a day devoted to honoring Max Samfield. Congregants and colleagues alike extolled the virtues of this unassuming rabbi, whose passionate commitment to community service had inspired two generations of Children of Israel, as well as many others, to strive for the betterment of humanity.

The news of Samfield's death elicited an outpouring of sorrow from every corner of Memphis, as well as from Jewish communities across the country. Every local newspaper published an editorial that praised his life of community service and his heroism during the yellow fever epidemics. Baron Hirsch Congregation held a special service in his memory, as did the Masonic Lodge. Many local businesses closed for ten minutes on the morning of Samfield's funeral. And in a rare gesture of admiration, the Memphis Street Railway Company cut off its power during the rabbi's funeral, causing every streetcar in town to come to a halt for a full minute.[46]

That the citizens of Memphis found it in their hearts to honor Samfield in this way is testimony to their generosity of spirit. That they did so at this particular time in history — just six weeks after Leo Frank, a Jewish citizen of Atlanta, was hanged by a lynch mob in Marietta, Georgia, after having been unjustly convicted of murder — speaks volumes about the level of respect that existed in Memphis for Congregation Children of Israel and its revered rabbi.

Thus one era ended for Children of Israel, and an exciting new one began.

JOSEPH NEWBURGER
Congregation President, 1915-1926

In May 1916, led by its new senior rabbi, William Fineshriber, and a new president, Joseph Newburger, the congregation moved a mile and three-quarters east to its stately new home at the corner of Poplar and Montgomery, achieving the goal that former president Herman Gronauer had set some ten years earlier.

Newburger, a dapper gentleman who had moved to Memphis in 1896 from Coffeeville, Mississippi, was by all accounts a business genius, and in his day he was perhaps the most prominent cotton man in the South. In 1912 Newburger was reported by *The Commercial Appeal* to have "made a clear million dollars" on a single cotton deal.[47] That was the year he began building his large home on the southeast corner of East Parkway and Union Avenue, a residence described in the newspaper at the time as "a small castle."[48] (The building, modeled after *Le Petit Trianon* on the grounds of Versailles, later became the home of the Memphis Theological Seminary.)

A regular worshipper at Children of Israel's Friday night services, Newburger also belonged to Baron Hirsch Congregation, and he was a director of the Federation of Jewish Welfare Agencies and the National Board of Jewish War Relief. His philanthropy, much of which was dedicated to his daughters, Joy and Mary, also benefited many non-Jewish organizations; among these was the Memphis Community

WILLIAM FINESHRIBER
Spiritual Leader of Children of Israel, 1915-1924

Fund, to which he was the largest single contributor for many years.[49] As president of Children of Israel for eleven years, Newburger piloted the congregation during World War I and the period of financial difficulties that followed it. And in 1916, it was his privilege to lead Congregation Children of Israel into its new home.

Designed to resemble the celebrated Santa Sofia Mosque in Istanbul, the new house of worship at Poplar and Montgomery featured a great central dome, flanked by two smaller domes on either side. Etched in stone above the three pairs of front doors were the words, "Thou Shalt Love Thy Neighbor As

The Temple at Poplar Avenue and Montgomery Street, dedicated by the congregation in May 1916.

Inside the sanctuary at Poplar and Montgomery

Thyself." Inside the twelve-hundred-seat sanctuary, the pulpit was richly paneled in fruitwood, and above the paneling stood the huge pipes of a $10,000 organ. The instrument was a gift to the congregation from the Ladies Auxiliary, whose members had raised most of the money by preparing home-cooked meals, carrying them on the streetcar, and selling them to customers downtown. The new Temple also boasted fourteen well-lighted classrooms — a feature Rabbi Samfield surely would have appreciated — and an auditorium with a stage.

The dedication ceremonies, preceded by a

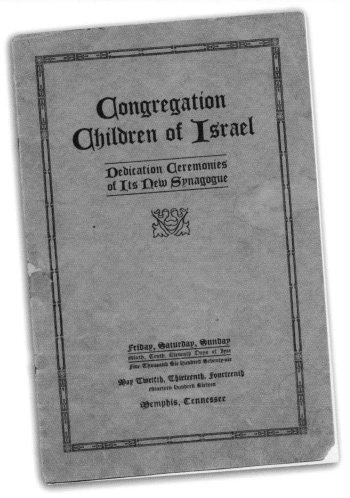

Program from the 1916 Dedication Ceremonies

Fineshriber vowed the new facility would be a house of God not only for all Jews, but also for anyone else who wanted to cross its threshold. "The only card of admission to [this] Temple is the belief of those who enter in 'walking humbly before the Lord our God,'" he declared, "and the adherence to the precepts of the nineteenth chapter of Leviticus engraved over the doorway of the Temple entrance." Topping off the dedication weekend, the Ladies Auxiliary put on a "musicale." Mrs. Mark Davis, Mrs. Hirsch Morris, and Mrs. Joseph Rosenfield took the podium to convey the Auxiliary's best wishes and to dedicate the organ to the memory of Rabbi Samfield.[50]

Now that the congregation was happily ensconced in its new house of worship, just one matter relating to the old Temple remained unresolved: the building had yet to be sold. In August 1916, President Joseph Newburger called a special meeting to report that he had received an offer from Beth El Emeth, a new Orthodox congregation that was being organized under the same name as the one that had disbanded in 1882. Curiously, not everyone was in favor of selling the building to this particular buyer. C. J. Haase, who spoke out against the sale, argued that in light of the congregation's twenty-year relationship with Baron Hirsch, Children of Israel should not assist the new congregation, which would compete with Baron Hirsch for members. Haase's comments sparked a lengthy discussion among the trustees, but in the end they did extend a helping hand to Beth El Emeth. They gave the new congregation the use of the old Poplar Temple for the High Holy Days in 1916, and in November of that year they accepted Beth El Emeth's offer to buy the building for $2,500 in cash, plus $12,000 payable in monthly installments. The following year, when Beth El Emeth became delinquent in its payments, Joseph Newburger urged the Board to "indulge our

farewell service held a week earlier at the old Poplar Avenue Temple, stretched over an entire weekend in May 1916. Sam Schloss, Sam Hirsch, and Jacob Goldsmith drew the honor of carrying the Torahs into the new sanctuary, and Solomon Sternberg, the privilege of kindling the everlasting light above the ark. Guest speakers included Rabbi William Rosenau, president of the Central Conference of American Rabbis; Dr. Henry Berkowitz, a prominent Reform rabbi from Philadelphia; and Rabbi Abram Brill of Meridian, Mississippi. In his own remarks, Rabbi brethren" and be as lenient as possible.

Meanwhile, Children of Israel was flourishing under Rabbi Fineshriber's leadership. Youthful and energetic, the rabbi was considered a breath of fresh air by the congregation, especially in his role as head of the religious school. "While small in physique, he is tremendously large in optimism and enthusiasm," Sabbath School Committee Chairman Leon Sternberger wrote of Fineshriber as early as 1914. "Dr. Fineshriber understands the nature and disposition of children . . . and above all has the patience and versatility to adapt . . . to their every requirement."

Fineshriber's energy, combined with the excitement of being in the splendid new building, sparked a renewal of interest among the members, and the years following his installation as senior rabbi in 1915 were marked by a number of "firsts." The first scout troop sponsored by the congregation — Boy Scout Troop 25 — was organized in 1915; the interdenominational troop would still be meeting at Temple Israel more than eighty-five years later.

The first post-Confirmation class was formed in 1916, and the first outdoor *sukkah* was constructed in 1917, funded by Jacob Goldsmith in honor of the fiftieth anniversary of his arrival in Memphis. In June 1918 a historic "first" took place when the congregation voted to make all seats in the sanctuary "free and unassigned." And in 1921 the Junior Congregation, forerunner of the Memphis Federation of Temple Youth (MeFTY), was established.

During this period, the congregation continued to liberalize its religious customs. As in the past, proposed changes were discussed openly at congregational meetings and required a majority vote to be adopted. During one such meeting the members approved another modification of their funeral practices. Henceforth, it was decided, family members and other mourners would be encouraged to depart from the grave before the coffin was lowered into the ground and covered, rather than staying, as had been customary in the past, to shovel the first layer of earth themselves.

One change that did not receive a majority vote was a proposal made back in 1912 to abolish the ceremony of bar mitzvah. By then, this traditional rite of passage for thirteen-year-old Jewish boys had been almost totally eclipsed in Reform congregations by Confirmation, the

Boy Scout Troop 25, circa 1929:
FRONT ROW (LEFT TO RIGHT): *James Sweeney, Saul Perlman, Max Weis, Jimmy Haimsohn, Bernard Michel;* **BACK ROW:** *J.G. Griesbeck, Ezra Krivcher, Henry Lehman, Louis Weis, Charles Griesbeck.*

ceremony in which fifteen-year-old boys — and girls — affirm their faith as a group. In this case, however, tradition won out over modernization. On a motion by Herman Bluthenthal, the congregation opted to retain bar mitzvahs for the few members who still wanted them.

At the annual meeting in May 1916, the first to be held in the new Temple, the members resolved to make three important and lasting changes: they discontinued observing the eighth day of Sukkot and Pesach; they initiated the practice of having the rabbi read the names of those whose *yahrtzeits* were being observed each week and of requiring all worshippers, not just the mourners, to stand for the reciting of the *Kaddish*; and they revived the Orthodox custom, apparently eliminated somewhere along the way, of naming and blessing babies during services.

In addition, the members approved a motion that day to enlarge the Sunday School Committee by inviting a few women to join its ranks; the action marked the first time in the history of the congregation that women were permitted to have an official voice, apart from the Ladies Auxiliary, in its affairs. Whether by coincidence or design, the members also voted that day to establish a Men's Auxiliary — although, for some reason, such a group was not actually formed until 1926.

Among the most enduring "firsts" of the Fineshriber years was the introduction of a monthly bulletin, which the rabbi himself edited. The inaugural issue, dated November 1915, sketched a vivid portrait of congregational life at the time. "Do you know that we have organized a Class in Hebrew, which any child or adult may join?" Fineshriber wrote in a column headlined, appropriately, "Do You Know?" "Do you know that we have a beautiful and impressive Children's Service, participated in by over 400 people, every Sunday morning at 10:20, under the direction of Leon Sternberger?" Next to the "Do You Know?" column was the roster of religious school teachers for the 1915-16 school year: Mrs. Harry Lewis, Mrs. M.J. Vosse, Leah Levy, Sarah Lewine, Selma R. Cohn, Rosa Levy, Mrs. O.S. Benham, Aimee Halle, Abe Waldauer, Mrs. Albert J. Fink, and Lelia and Helene Samfield, two of Rabbi Samfield's three daughters. (Samfield and his wife also had four sons.)

At the time this bulletin was published, Europe had already been at war for more than a year, and German submarines were posing a serious threat to any ship crossing the Atlantic Ocean. Just six months earlier a German submarine had sunk the Cunard passenger ship *Lusitania*, and 128 Americans were among the dead. While Rabbi Fineshriber did not address the international situation directly in November 1915, he did hold forth on such issues as "What Constitutes an American?" and "Is there Anti-Semitism in America?" With the world in turmoil, the rabbi of Children of Israel was apparently starting to ask the uneasy question that always gnaws at the Jewish people in times of trouble: "How is this going to affect us as Jews?"

A year and a half later, after German submarines sank several American merchant ships, the United States finally was forced to take action. On April 2, 1917, President Woodrow Wilson delivered a war message to Congress, declaring, "The world must be made safe for democracy," and four days later, on April 6, Congress declared war on Germany.

Along with the rest of the nation, Congregation Children of Israel turned its attention from everyday, parochial concerns to the bloody battles that were raging in France and Belgium and to the young men from here who would soon be joining the fight, as the title of a popular song put it, "Over There." The Temple building was draped in red, white, and blue for an entire month, and in the religious school,

Mrs. Julius Goodman staged a series of patriotic programs every Sunday. The children and their teachers directed their weekly charity contributions to go to the War Sufferers Fund, Belgian Babies Outfits, French War Orphans, and other relief organizations.[51] And 131 young men from Congregation Children of Israel — out of a total membership of about 450 families — voluntarily joined or were drafted into military service. One member, James Nathan, Jr., was killed.

World War I ended on November 11, 1918, and in the decade that followed, Americans turned their backs on the liberalism and internationalism of President Woodrow Wilson, opting instead for the "return to normalcy" promised by Warren G. Harding, who was elected president in 1920. For the members of Children of Israel, that meant focusing their attention once more on the need to retire the $28,000 debt they had assumed in order to build the new Temple. Dave Sternberg, the congregation's treasurer, vowed he would find a way to accomplish that goal.

In the meantime, in 1922 the Board decided to train a group of young men for leadership in the congregation by establishing a Junior Board. The first group of appointees, an able and accomplished collection of young professionals and businessmen, included many who would later serve as officers and trustees of the congregation: Dr. Gilbert S. Levy, Dr. Neuton Stern, Merrill Jacobs, Abe D. Waldauer, Charles W. Myers, Sidney Allenberg, Myron Halle, Elias Goldsmith, Sr., A. Arthur Halle, Joseph D. Marks, E. Klein, A.B. Lewis, and Gilbert M. Schloss. Also recruited for that first Junior

Board were two men who developed a special relationship with the congregation: Henry J. Lewis, who would serve as the congregation's executive director from 1951 to 1965, and an up-and-coming young businessman named Abe Plough, the founder of Plough, Inc. (later Schering-Plough), who would go on to become the largest benefactor in the congregation's history.

HENRY J. LEWIS
Executive Director, 1951-1965

On the national scene, two new amendments to the Constitution were ratified after the war. The Eighteenth Amendment, which prohibited the manufacture and distribution of liquor, required the congregation to appoint a custodian of the

---

GENERAL MEETING OF THE CONGREGATION "CHILDREN OF ISRAEL"

Notice is hereby given that a Special-General Meeting of the congregation will be held in the Sunday School Auditorium of the Temple on

SUNDAY, JUNE 6th, 1920, AT 5:00 P. M.

This meeting is in lieu of the Regular Annual Meeting and is called to consider and dispose of all matters which might lawfully be considered by or brought before the regular annual meeting, including the election of Officers and Trustees for the ensuing year, the submission and disposition of the reports of officers and any other business that may properly come before the meeting.

Notice is also hereby given that the following amendment of the By-Laws will be submitted for action:

"That Article VI, Section 1, of the Constitution and By-Laws, as amended, be amended so as to make the same read as follows:

"Section 1. The Annual Meeting of the Congregation shall be held on the first Sunday in June, each year, when the election of officers will take place, and the fiscal year of the congregation shall begin on the first day of May and terminate on the 30th day of April, and all accounts shall be kept accordingly."

LADIES INVITED AND SUPPER SERVED

Putting into effect the recommendation of the President at the Annual Meeting last year, which was adopted by the congregation, the ladies of the congregation are invited to attend the meeting and to participate in the discussion of congregational affairs, and by their presence and otherwise help to make the Annual Meeting an event of real importance.

Supper will be served immediately after the conclusion of the business meeting.

I. DINKELSPIEL, *Secretary*.

By order of the President.

sacramental wine; Sam Slager, the sexton, got the job.[52] The Nineteenth Amendment, ratified in August of 1920, gave women the right to vote.

Not to be outdone, Congregation Children of Israel also gave women the right to vote in 1920. Following a recommendation by President Newburger that women be allowed to participate in all future congregational meetings, the notice of the 1920 annual meeting contained not one, but two inducements for members to attend: "LADIES INVITED AND SUPPER SERVED." At the meeting, President Newburger offered a warm welcome to the ladies and appointed three of them to serve on a committee charged with figuring out how to eliminate the congregation's debt. The records indicate, however, that three more years went by before a woman actually found the courage to speak out at an annual meeting. The first to do so was Hattie Brooks, who pointed out in 1923 that the cemetery grounds should be "more carefully looked after" and recommended that a committee of ladies should be formed to assist the Cemetery Committee in this work. Newburger, never one to ignore a good suggestion, appointed five women to serve on such a committee, under the chairmanship of the intrepid Mrs. Brooks.

Rabbi Fineshriber himself had been an early advocate of women's suffrage and was one of the first men in the Memphis area to speak out on the subject. At a "Suffragette Day" rally on May 1, 1914, he told a crowd of fifteen hundred people assembled in Court Square: "[The] purpose of this meeting . . . is to shock the people of Memphis into a realization that the question of equal suffrage is not child's play . . . . Woman seeking the right to vote has the backing of the best element among men and of the church."[53]

Fineshriber, a powerful and persuasive lecturer, was known for his ability to speak without notes. "You could wake him out of a sound sleep and ask him to speak on Einstein's Theory of Relativity and he would charm you with what he had to say," said Dr. Julian B. Feibelman, who served as an assistant to Fineshriber later in his career.[54] Greatly in demand as a public speaker, the rabbi's topics ran the gamut from literary reviews ("Bernard Shaw and the Modernist Movement," "Rudyard Kipling's Poetry," "Eugene O'Neill's *Beyond the Horizon*"), to matters of Jewish concern ("The Jews of Egypt and Syria"), to such hot political issues as tariff revisions and the cancellation of German war reparations, both of which he favored. He was never one to shy away from controversy. In this ultra-conservative, Bible-belt community, Fineshriber spoke out vehemently against blue laws. "To attempt to legislate goodness and religion into society," he asserted, "is vicious in its conception and damnable in its results."[55]

In 1922, when a group of fundamentalist Christians, led by former Secretary of State William Jennings Bryan, began crusading for a ban on the teaching of evolution in public schools and universities, Fineshriber devoted three successive Friday nights to a discussion of Darwin's theory of evolution. Nearly nine hundred people turned out to hear the series of three sermons, filling the main floor of the sanctuary at Poplar and Montgomery and spilling over into the balcony.

Fineshriber launched the series by reminding his audience about the "inalienable right of free thought and free speech, guaranteed by the Constitution of the United States."[56] Then he got to the heart of the matter. "The majority of thoughtful and liberal preachers of the world have found no difficulty in accepting the theory of evolution without discarding their Bibles or their religion," he said. "You can worship God only in the light of truth; God grant that we shall not lock the gates of our universities to the men who are seekers after the truth, [nor] put blinders on our instructors and our students. We heed what our physicians say, we heed what our learned men of the law say, and we give the words of statesmen due weight. Why, then, should the men of science alone remain unhonored in America?"[57] Though warmly received by the congregation, Fineshriber's lectures did nothing to stem the tide of fundamentalism in Tennessee. Three years after he delivered these sermons, Tennessee became the first state in the nation to enact a law that banned the teaching of evolution in public schools. (The law was challenged in court in the notorious Scopes "Monkey Trial," which later became the focus of a play and a movie called *Inherit the Wind*, but Tennessee's ban on teaching evolution was not repealed until 1967.)

Most of all, however, Rabbi Fineshriber is remembered in Memphis for having the courage to speak out — when virtually no one else did — against racism and bigotry, and especially against lynching. His voice was first heard on the subject on May 22, 1917, after a black man who had been accused of raping and murdering a white girl was brutally killed by a mob in Memphis — burned alive, in fact — in front of an estimated fifteen thousand witnesses. Local newspapers had reported for several days that an atrocity such as this might take place, but no one, apparently, spoke out against it.

Sickened by what had happened, Rabbi Fineshriber called a meeting of the congregation that very day and told the members, "We ought to be the first to state publicly what we think about the horrible thing of burning a Negro."[58] The rabbi contacted his friend, *Commercial Appeal* editor C.P.J. Mooney, and urged Mooney to publish an editorial on the subject. The following day's *Commercial Appeal* carried an account of the congregation's condemnation of lynching, and the editorial against lynching — an extremely

timid protest, given the circumstances — appeared two days later, on May 25. That day's newspaper also carried a statement from a group of Protestant, Catholic, and Jewish clergy confessing they had neglected their duty by not speaking out sooner against mob violence.[59]

In the following years Fineshriber continued to speak out against racial prejudice and discrimination, and in 1921 he even took on the Ku Klux Klan, which was on the rise in Memphis at the time. Boldly, Fineshriber announced his intention to "preach on the KKK" in *The Commercial Appeal* on October 14, 1921.[60] That evening he did so, denouncing the Klan from the pulpit at Poplar and Montgomery as "an organized mob" that fostered the survival of Anglo-Saxons in America to the exclusion of all other Americans. "Let us pray," the rabbi said, "that the world has been sufficiently enlightened through the great struggle of war

to make us realize that might is not right, and that the glamour of a white robe does not take the place of justice meted out through the regular channels of law in the courts . . . . The policy of the Ku Klux Klan would tear down order and substitute mob law. . . . It is a menace to the principles of Americans and far more dangerous than Bolshevism."[61]

It was Fineshriber's condemnation of the Klan, so bravely and boldly expressed, that gave others in Memphis the courage to follow suit. In 1922 *The Commercial Appeal* published a series of editorials against the Klan and exposed it to ridicule in front-page cartoons by J.P. Alley; the coordinated campaign earned the newspaper a Pulitzer Prize in 1923. And some of the city's other clergymen — Episcopal Bishop Thomas F. Gailor, among others — criticized the Klan as well.[62] But it was Fineshriber who was the first to stick his neck out.

Years later, in an interview with historian Berkley Kalin, the rabbi acknowledged that his denunciation of the Klan in 1921 had caused plenty of anxiety within his family. When his younger brother came to Memphis for a visit that year, Fineshriber recalled, he warned the rabbi, "This is a very dangerous thing you are doing," and insisted on giving him a pistol to use for protection. "I still have the pistol," Fineshriber, then eighty-nine, told Kalin with a chuckle. "I haven't used it, but I still have it."[63]

Fineshriber was the spiritual leader of Children of Israel for only nine years. In the spring of 1924 he received a call to become the rabbi of Keneseth-Israel Congregation in Philadelphia, the largest Reform congregation in the nation at the time. Although President Newburger immediately dispatched a delegation of the congregation's leaders — Milton Binswanger, Sr., M.H. Rosenthal, and Elias Gates — to try to talk Fineshriber out of leaving, the rabbi was firm in his decision, as Gates later reported, that "his future lay in a larger field." The congregation had no choice but to accept Fineshriber's resignation, effective August 31, 1924.

When the news of his resignation spread, both daily newspapers published editorials in Fineshriber's honor. "Few men have been more closely identified with the moral and intellectual advancement of the community and the promotion of worthy and deserving enterprises," the *News-Scimitar* wrote on March 30, 1924. "He is a strong champion of justice and fair play. All men would be better if they would keep before them the ideals that he has as his standard."[64]

Characteristically, Fineshriber continued to be a lightning rod for controversy throughout his career in Philadelphia. In 1942 he helped found the American Council for Judaism, the most prominent anti-Zionist organization in the country, and his vocal and consistent support of that group eventually brought him into conflict with the leadership of the Union of American Hebrew Congregations. At Children of Israel, however, Fineshriber is remembered as a champion of literary scholarship and freedom of thought, and most of all, as a leader whose courageous advocacy of social justice would inspire all future rabbis of the congregation. Fineshriber, who retired from Keneseth-Israel in 1949, remained in Philadelphia for the rest of his life and died there in 1968. He is the only senior rabbi in Temple Israel's history who, upon his death, was not buried in the Temple's cemetery.

At this point in its history, Congregation Children of Israel — now about 650 families strong — swapped rabbis, in a sense, with the Reform Jews of Philadelphia.

Rabbi Fineshriber went to Keneseth-Israel Congregation in Philadelphia, and the Rev. Dr. Harry W. Ettelson, formerly of Philadelphia's Rodeph Shalom Congregation, accepted a call to Memphis.

Ettelson, who was born and raised in Mobile, Alabama, was the first native Southerner to occupy the congregation's pulpit. Intellectual and erudite, the new rabbi had the air and the academic credentials of a college professor: Bachelor of Arts with honors from the University of Cincinnati, graduate work at the University of Chicago, and a Ph.D. in languages from Yale. At Hebrew Union College, where he received his ordination, Ettelson was the valedictorian of his class.

In contrast to his predecessors, who were in their twenties or thirties when they arrived in Memphis, Ettelson was forty-one when he assumed the pulpit of Children of Israel, a seasoned rabbi who had been a Navy chaplain during World War I and who had already served Reform congregations in Ft. Wayne, Indiana, and Hartford, Connecticut, in addition to Philadelphia. He and his wife, Nell, arrived in Memphis in the spring of 1925 to a warm welcome from the congregation, which had been without a permanent spiritual leader since Fineshriber's departure eight months earlier. On April 2, 1925, the couple attended a dinner in their honor at Ridgeway Country Club, hosted by the

HARRY W. ETTELSON
Spiritual Leader of Temple Israel, 1925-1954

trustees and their wives. The following evening Ettelson was installed as the fifth rabbi in Children of Israel's history.

"Come now, let us make a Covenant — I and thou!" the new rabbi declared in his inaugural sermon from the pulpit at Poplar and Montgomery. "Whenever . . . rabbi and congregation form a Covenant, they have [in] back of their individual compact the inspiration of the original Covenant, enriched by all the hallowed traditions, heroism, martyrdoms, and ideals of the centuries . . . . They are giving mutual pledges of loyalty to the heritage of the past — the age-old principles of the faith — only interpreted in the living terms of present-day duties, responsibilities, needs, and opportunities. Come, then, let us make a Covenant!"[65]

So began the Ettelson years at Children of Israel, a twenty-nine year period that would mark the high point of the congregation's adherence to what has come to be known as Classical Reform Judaism. Classical Reform, as articulated in the eight-point Pittsburgh Platform adopted by the Central Conference of American Rabbis in 1885 (and modified in 1937), asserted the right of Jews to disregard all laws and ceremonies that were "not adapted to the views and habits of modern civilization"; declared that Jews were "no longer a nation," but a religious community with a shared history and a common faith; eliminated the concept of a personal Messiah, substituting instead the ideal of a Messianic age that would establish "a kingdom of truth, justice, and peace among all men"; extended the hand of fellowship "to all who cooperate with us in the establishment of the reign of truth and righteousness among men"; and deemed it the sacred duty of Jews "to solve . . . the problems presented by the contrasts and evils of the present organization of society."

Like other Reform congregations across the nation — especially those in the South — Children of Israel had enthusiastically embraced the principles of the Pittsburgh Platform. Over time its worship services had taken on American overtones, and ritual and tradition had taken a back seat to the ethical teachings of the prophets. One verse from the prophet Micah had become especially popular: "It hath been told thee what is good and what the Lord doth require of thee — only to do justly, to love mercy, and to walk humbly with thy God."

By the time of Ettelson's arrival, there were no bar mitzvahs at Congregation Children of Israel, no obligation to observe the ancient dietary laws, no participation by congregants in the reading of the Torah, no cantor to chant the traditional Hebrew prayers. With a few exceptions — notably the *Shema,* the *Barechu,* the *Vaanachnu* (which had come to be known as "the Adoration"), and the Mourner's *Kaddish* — the members generally prayed in English. They sang in English, too. While services still concluded on occasion with a rousing rendition of *Ein Keiloheinu,* many of the old Hebrew stand-bys had given way to such hymns as "We Meet Again in Gladness" and "God is in His Holy Temple."

Worship services at the Temple at Poplar and Montgomery were carried out with dignity, and with an emphasis on rabbinical performance over congregational participation. Ettelson's sermons, described by congregants as "scholarly" and "cerebral," often dwelled on the universal mission of the Jewish people to bring peace and justice to the world through community service, a model for behavior that came to be known as "social action."

Like Fineshriber, Ettelson believed the Temple should be "a house of God for all people"; thus the prevailing spirit at Children of Israel was ecumenical. In 1925, having promised in his inaugural sermon that he would try "to establish fraternal relations and the fullest neighborly contacts with the ministers of all denominations," Ettelson organized the Cross-Cut Club, a group of local clergymen who sponsored a non-sectarian Thanksgiving service and a number of other interfaith programs. The club formed the nucleus of the Memphis chapter of the National Conference of Christians and Jews when it was founded in 1932.

While there were few if any modifications of ritual during Ettelson's twenty-nine year tenure, congregational life was far from static; as times changed, so too did Children of Israel. In 1925, for example, a long-standing tradition was broken when the Sisterhood won permission, via an amendment to the bylaws, to elect two women annually to sit on the Board of Trustees alongside the fourteen men elected by the congregation at large. Effie Greener, then president of the Sisterhood, and Beulah Vosse, who later became the principal of the religious school, were the first women to get the nod. It would take twenty-four more years, however, for a woman to be included on the slate of trustees elected by the congregation as a whole. The first to achieve that honor, in 1949, was Mildred Haas.

MILDRED HAAS
The first woman elected to Temple Israel's Board of Trustees

Ettelson's second year with the congregation, 1926, was eventful for a number of reasons. The Temple Men's Club (forerunner of the Brotherhood) was established that year, under the leadership of Dr. Louis Levy, president; William Goodman and B.W. Hirsh, vice presidents; Lloyd Bensinger, treasurer; and Eugene Lerner, secretary. The organization, which attracted some two hundred members during its first year, featured well-known speakers, both Jewish and non-Jewish, at its meetings. It soon became affiliated with the National Federation

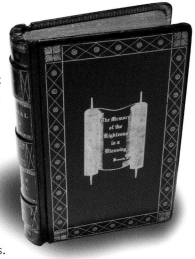

of Temple Brotherhoods. That same year, at Ettelson's suggestion, the congregation established the Memorial Book, in which members could have the names of deceased relatives and friends inscribed, ensuring that their loved ones would be remembered by the congregation every year, in perpetuity, on their *yahrtzeits*. The Memorial Book was dedicated to the memory of Sam Schloss, the last surviving charter member of Children of Israel, and his wife, Sarah. Born in Germany in 1834, Schloss had come to Memphis in 1852 — two years before the congregation was formed — and was still serving as its vice president when he died in 1925, a month short of his ninety-first birthday.

Also in 1926 the congregation embarked on yet another building project — this time to enlarge the religious school, which had outgrown its space in the new Temple in just eleven years. To finance the construction of an addition that would accommodate about three hundred students, President Joseph Newburger donated $12,000 — about half the amount needed — and the congregation borrowed the rest.

The Joy and Mary Newburger Religious School Annex, named for Newburger's daughters, was dedicated in December 1926.

Joseph Newburger passed away just a few weeks later, at the age of sixty-eight. Inspired by his devotion to community service, the congregation for some years afterward awarded a Joseph Newburger Cup to the member who was judged to have done the most for the community.

After Newburger's death, Vice President Leon Sternberger, who had served for many years as chairman of the Religious School Committee, moved up to the presidency. He held the office until October 1928, when he retired due to ill health. A modest and unassuming man who was at first hesitant to follow in Newburger's footsteps, Sternberger tackled his responsibilities with a rare sense of compassion and thoughtfulness: while he was president he took it upon himself to make a personal visit to every member of the congregation who was ill.[66] Under Sternberger's leadership the congregation completely revised its constitution and bylaws, paid off the loan for the Religious School Annex, and instituted a better system to manage its finances.

LEON STERNBERGER
Congregation President, 1926-1928

Sternberger was succeeded in 1928 by Milton S. Binswanger, Sr., who had chaired the Building Committee during the construction of the Temple at Poplar and Montgomery. Binswanger, the president of Binswanger Glass Co. and all its branches, also took on the presidency with

MILTON BINSWANGER, SR.
Congregation President, 1928-1930

some reluctance; he declined the nomination when his name was first put forth, but the congregation disregarded his protests and elected him anyway, by acclamation.

As president, Binswanger's first item of business was to purchase the house directly south of the Temple, a structure the congregation planned to use as a meeting place for the Junior Congregation. While the Board planned to borrow the $7,250 it would take to purchase the property, the house needed to be remodeled, and Binswanger hoped to finance those costs with donations. Meanwhile, the new president was also looking for money for another project. Over the previous few months the Board had received a number of requests — from Gaston Meyer of Earle, Arkansas, and H. Borstein of Wynne, Arkansas, among others — for the congregation to broadcast its Friday evening worship services on the radio. Ettelson heartily approved of the idea and was pushing to have the arrangements made in time for the congregation's seventy-fifth anniversary celebration in the spring of 1929.

The solution to both problems lay in the generosity of just one man. He was identified at the time simply as

"an anonymous donor," but later on, under the pseudonym "Mr. Anonymous," he became widely recognized as the Mid-South's most outstanding philanthropist, Abe Plough. In his first, but by no means his last, significant gift to the congregation, Plough quietly footed the bill for both projects.

The broadcasting equipment was installed just in time to air the congregation's grand — and very lengthy —"Diamond Jubilee" services on Friday, April 5, 1929. Those who tuned in to station WNBR that night, as well as those who attended in person, were treated to a program that included two organ selections performed by Effie Oppenheimer; four anthems sung by the choir; twelve pages of "Sabbath Eve Devotions" from the *Union Prayer Book*; greetings from congregation President Milton Binswanger, Sr.; an invocation by the Rev. Dr. David Philipson, president of Hebrew Union College in Cincinnati; comments on "The Significance of the Charter," by Elias Gates, a member of the Board of Trustees; "Fellowship Greetings from the City Churches," delivered by Episcopal Bishop Thomas F. Gailor; and not one, but *two* major speeches — a "Jubilee Address" by Dr. Ettelson, and an "Anniversary Sermon" delivered by the congregation's former rabbi, Dr. William Fineshriber.

Chaired by Vice President David Asher Levy, the celebration continued throughout that weekend. There was another special worship service on Saturday morning, a Diamond Jubilee Banquet held at The Peabody hotel on Saturday evening (which featured its own lineup of twelve speakers, as well as a choral selection, before the dancing began), and a program for the religious school on Sunday morning. In addition, the congregation published a booklet that chronicled Children of Israel's seventy-five year history, written by Babette M. Becker and illustrated by Louise Kornik.

EFFIE OPPENHEIMER
Temple Israel's choir director and organist, 1913-1953

By this time Children of Israel had a membership of nearly 750 families, and when the congregation gathered for its annual meeting in 1929, President Binswanger said he believed the time had come to stop seeking new members. "It is better to develop strength from within," he suggested, "than to endeavor to serve a greater number with smaller individual benefits."

Whether or not the members agreed with Binswanger, one thing was certain: collectively and individually, the congregation would need plenty of strength in the years to come. Tuesday, October 29, the day the 1929 annual meeting took place, was the notorious "Black Tuesday," the day the stock market crashed, bringing an abrupt end to the period of peace and prosperity known as the Roaring Twenties. Over the next twenty years the world would endure the devastating effects of the Great Depression and the chaos and destruction of World War II, in which an estimated fifty-five million people would die, including six million Jews murdered by the Nazis. It also would witness, in 1948, the establishment of the State of Israel.

In Memphis, Congregation Children of Israel would be profoundly touched by all these colossal events: it would tighten its belt in response to the hard economic times; send hundreds of its young men off to war, some of them never to return; welcome refugees from Nazi Germany into its midst; and struggle to reconcile the generally non-Zionist outlook of Classical Reform with the urgent need and compelling demand for a Jewish homeland in Palestine.

The job of piloting the congregation through the worst of the economic difficulties fell to Dr. Louis Levy, the founder of the Memphis Eye, Ear, Nose, and Throat Hospital, who was elected to succeed Binswanger in 1930 and held the presidency until 1937. As the annual income from dues fell from a high of about $47,000 in 1928-29 to a low of about $23,000 in 1932, Levy and the congregation's treasurer, Ben Goodman, Sr., struggled to keep the congregation afloat. Board meetings

Dr. Louis Levy
Congregation President, 1930-1937

during the period focused almost entirely on financial matters, as the trustees wrestled with painful budgetary decisions — including the implementation of across-the-board salary cuts — and repeatedly borrowed from the Cemetery Fund to make ends meet. In 1931 Dr. Ettelson voluntarily cut his own salary by $1,000 "for as long as present conditions persist and require it." Two years later, as the Depression dragged on, he asked the Board to cut his salary again, this time by 10 percent. "Times have been hard — times are still hard," President Levy lamented in his 1931 annual report to the congregation. "We have naturally felt the effects of the Depression, both in numbers and income."

Still, Children of Israel kept up with its normal activities as best it could, especially with regard to the children. In 1931 Beulah Vosse succeeded Selma Cohn as principal of the religious school, and Merrill Kremer became chairman of the Religious School Committee. Working together, they arranged for Dr. Henry Englander of Hebrew Union College to come to Memphis to lead a teacher-training workshop. In 1934, children's services were held on Rosh Hashanah for the first time; they had been introduced on Yom Kippur a few years earlier.

As for the Junior Congregation, it positively flourished during the Depression. In 1933 the group had 189 paid members, a record high at the time; they attended classes on Sunday mornings and participated in a full schedule of social and cultural programs. Under the guidance of its principal, Edwin Sapinsley, Sr., the Junior Congregation sponsored a youth conference for the

JACOB GOLDSMITH
Honorary President, 1932-1933

entire Southeastern District in 1933, the first of its kind in the region. Considering the state of the economy, it was a rousing success: in addition to the local contingent, the conclave drew five rabbis and forty-seven delegates from twelve cities and seven states.

While subject to cutbacks, adult programming also continued during the Depression, and once in a while something special came along to add spice to the mix. Such an event took place in January 1932 when Dr. Ettelson publicly debated the issue, "Is Religion Necessary?" with none other than Clarence Darrow, the celebrated trial attorney and noted agnostic who had defended John Scopes a few years earlier in the notorious Scopes "Monkey Trial." The event drew a capacity crowd to the Auditorium downtown, and a portion of the proceeds was donated to B'nai B'rith. While neither man was declared the winner, the hometown crowd — as well as the local newspapers —

clearly sided with Ettelson.

Later that year the congregation paid a well-deserved tribute to one of its oldest members, Jacob Goldsmith. In addition to reelecting him warden, the position he had held since 1914, the members named the venerable retailer honorary president, "as a testimonial of the esteem in which he is held not only in our congregation, but also in the community." When Goldsmith died in 1933 at the age of eighty-one, the employees of J. Goldsmith & Sons donated money for a bronze plaque with his likeness to be placed in the vestibule of the Temple, with the inscription, "The crown of a good name exceeds them all." (The plaque was later moved to the Goldsmith Civic Garden Center.)

A year after Goldsmith's death the congregation elected another of its esteemed elders, Hardwig Peres, to the position of honorary president. Peres, whose father, Jacob, had been the congregation's first rabbi, supported a wide range of civic and Jewish causes, from the John Gaston Memorial Fund, which helped make possible the construction of

DR. ETTELSON

The Issue: 'Is Religion Necessary?'

★ ★ ★   ★ ★ ★

Dr. Ettelson Answered 'Yes!' When He Matched Beliefs With Clarence Darrow In A 1932 Memphis Debate

CLARENCE DARROW

THE STAGE HAD BEEN SET. Clarence Darrow, the renowned criminal lawyer, and Dr. Harry W. Ettelson, rabbi of the then Congregation Children of Israel in Memphis, were to debate on the subject: Is Religion Necessary? The date was Jan. 14, 1932. The place: Memphis, Tennessee.

Hundreds flocked to the downtown auditorium, many, of course, to see Darrow in action. The admitted agnostic and iconoclast who regarded Christianity merely as an ancient philosophy, was to match wits with Memphis' own Jewish scholar.

A native of Mobile, Dr. Ettelson had come to Memphis in 1925, the same year that Darrow had

• Religion is necessary because it gives us a faith to live by and a hope to die with.

• That great thinker, the redoubtable foe of the ecclesiastical authorities of his time — none other than Voltaire himself said: "If God did not exist, it would be necessary to invent him.'"

★ ★ ★

DR. ETTELSON said further:

"If Religion on its all too human side has been darkened and degraded at times by men's passions and prejudices, on its divine side it has been the most potent factor in man's ethical and spiritual strivings.

gives us the ultimate sanctions of duty. It postulates a God of truth and righteousness at the heart of things and thereby gives to the moral law a reality much in the realm of man's higher life, as natural law has for his physical being.

"Is Religion necessary, ladies and gentlemen? Yes indeed! It is necessary because man needs lofty ideals and noble principles, and Religion holds out the loftiest ideals and noblest principles imaginable both as to duties to self and duties to others; and not only does Religion hold out these ideals and principles but it fires the enthusiasm and energizes the will to carry them out and challenges him to do and dare.

HARDWIG PERES
Honorary President, 1934-1948

the old John Gaston Hospital, to the YMHA, of which he was a founder and its first president. In 1927 the city's afternoon newspaper, the *Memphis Press-Scimitar,* had named Peres "the most valued citizen of Memphis."

By 1936 the worst of the Depression was over. While it was a bit premature to proclaim, as President Franklin D. Roosevelt's campaign theme song did in 1936, that "Happy Days Are Here Again," times were gradually getting better. The congregation's membership, which had fallen to 629 in 1932-33, had climbed back up to around 650, and the Board, encouraged by the progress, began making plans for the future. Salaries were gradually restored. Maintenance and repair projects, having been deferred for several years, were once more on the drawing boards, and the Religious School Committee was authorized to hire a professional educator to supervise the school. In February 1936 the members of Children of Israel celebrated a proud moment in the life of the congregation, a mark of achievement that had seemed unreachable only a few years earlier: despite the economic hardships of the Depression, they somehow managed to make the final payment of $40,000 to retire the twenty-year mortgage on the Temple building.

Ironically, it was at this point in time, just as economic stability was being restored and congregational life was beginning to get back to normal, that dissension arose between Children of Israel's rabbi and its Board of Trustees. Whatever the source of the friction — the details are lost to history — apparently it was not something new. Ettelson had been aware for several years that a faction of the Board was not in his corner; as early as 1931, after a private discussion with President Levy, he had agreed to begin looking around for another position. Still, he stayed on after that, and six more years passed before Levy was forced to call a special meeting of the Board in April 1937 to deal with renewed rumblings of discontent.

Looking back from a distance of nearly seventy years, it is hard to know whether the outcome of that momentous meeting in April of '37 was carefully orchestrated, or if it came about spontaneously. Either way, it was surely one of the most nerve-wracking Board meetings in the congregation's history.

The trustees started out in executive session that night, discussing among themselves the question of whether to retain Ettelson as their spiritual leader. At some point they invited the rabbi into the room to address the Board. Ettelson, having read the handwriting on the wall, did not stay long. He took the opportunity to make a few remarks, tendered his resignation, and left. Then a strange thing happened. In the wake of Ettelson's departure, Levy informed the trustees — who were no doubt hoping the matter had been settled and they could all go home — that Ettelson's resignation did not, in fact, close the book on the matter. The Board still had to decide, he said, whether to *accept* the rabbi's resignation.

That, of course, put the whole divisive issue back on the table. During the lengthy discussion that followed, two or three trustees urged the Board to accept Ettelson's resignation, but quite a few more —

at least eight — spoke in favor of rejecting it. It was late in the evening when the question was finally called. By a vote of sixteen to seven, the Board resolved to reject Ettelson's resignation. The trustees gave Ettelson a vote of confidence and recommended that the members of Children of Israel reelect him as their rabbi at the next annual meeting.

The annual meeting took place on the first of June, by which time Ettelson had lined up a great deal of support. Recording Secretary Henry J. Lewis read a stack of telegrams and letters the Board had received in praise of the rabbi. After considerable discussion, during which the rabbi was absent from the room, the crucial vote was taken by secret ballot. The result was a landslide: by a vote of 303 to 31, the members chose to retain Harry W. Ettelson as their spiritual leader. "There was a tremendous ovation accorded the announcement," Henry Lewis wrote in the minutes. When Ettelson was invited back into the room, he expressed his "profound satisfaction and appreciation for this overwhelming vote of confidence." Not surprisingly, Lewis noted, the rabbi also expressed his "high esteem and affection" for President Levy.

So ended this tumultuous episode in the affairs of the congregation. Years later, a number of congregants who remembered the brouhaha said it was serious enough to have caused a split in the congregation. "In another congregation, in another city, that's what would have happened," one member suggested. But it did not happen at Children of Israel. Buoyed by the resounding vote of confidence, Ettelson stayed on as the spiritual leader of Children of Israel for seventeen more years, earning an abundance of respect and affection from the congregation and the community at large. In the aftermath of the conflict, Ettelson's supporters and detractors put their differences behind them and moved forward together. And the congregation as a whole drew strength from having weathered the storm.

Almost eclipsed by the drama that played out at the 1937 annual meeting was the election of officers that was held that night.

After seven taxing years as Children of Israel's president, Dr. Louis Levy retired from office, and the congregation elected Jacob C. Felsenthal to succeed him. Felsenthal, a wholesale grocer whose uncle, Bernard Felsenthal, was one of the founders of Reform Judaism in America, had moved to Memphis from Jackson, Tennessee, in 1918, prompted by business concerns and by his desire to provide a wider range of Jewish acquaintances for his children.

While it had been Levy's lot to resolve the dicey dilemma of whether to retain the rabbi, Felsenthal soon found himself with a different type of rabbi problem: no rabbi at all. Late in 1937 Ettelson experienced a recurrence of a throat ailment for which he had undergone surgery a few years earlier, and starting in January 1938 he took an eight-month leave of absence to rest his voice. During his earlier absence, which lasted for ten weeks, Ettelson had taken the unusual step of inviting prominent members of the Christian clergy to be guest speakers at services. "For some of the ministers it was a totally new experience to be in a Jewish house of worship," President Levy noted at the time. "They carried away with them and into their congregations an impression of Jewish values that [could be] a fine influence toward better understanding of the Jew and Judaism." This time, faced with a pulpit vacancy that would last more than

half a year, the Board looked around for another rabbi. Rabbi Morton J. Cohn, director of the Southwest District of the Union of American Hebrew Congregations, was hired initially just to fill in for Ettelson during his absence, but in May 1938 Cohn accepted an offer to stay on with the congregation as "junior rabbi" and director of the religious school after Ettelson's return. From this time on, except for a few transition periods, the congregation would always employ at least two rabbis.

Meanwhile, a new and very serious worry had begun to creep into the consciousness of the members of Children of Israel: in January 1933, Adolph Hitler and his Nazi Party had seized control of Germany, and in the months that followed, the position of Germany's Jewish citizens had become precarious.

At the annual meeting in October

JACOB C. FELSENTHAL
Congregation President, 1937-1939

1933, just nine months after Hitler came to power, the members received a first-hand report on the civil rights abuses of the Third Reich from Rabbi Julius Mark, spiritual leader of the Vine Street Temple in Nashville, who had visited Germany the previous summer. A sizeable crowd — "probably the largest attendance in years," according to the minutes — turned out to hear Mark's address, a chilling account of the predicament of the Jews in Nazi Germany. The rabbi's speech was "extremely interesting," Henry Lewis wrote later, "but unfortunately revolting."

Throughout the 1930s, as the situation in Germany grew ever more dangerous, the congregation did what little it could — on its own, in concert with other Jewish groups, and as individuals — to try to help Germany's Jews. As early as June 1933, the Board sent a telegram to Secretary of State Cordell Hull voicing its concern about the treatment Jews were receiving in Germany. By September 1938, their concern had turned to alarm. Just before the High Holy Days, Herbert Herff, M.A. Lightman, Sr., and William Goodman asked the Board for permission to make an unprecedented appeal during Rosh Hashanah services for funds to help Jews get out of Germany. In light of the urgency of the situation, the Board approved their request.

It was just two months later that Hitler's henchmen carried out the infamous rampage of death and destruction known as *Kristallnacht* (Night of Broken Glass). When news of that attack reached Memphis, it prompted an outpouring of sympathy and support from the Christian clergy, led by Episcopal Bishop James M. Maxon, who helped organize a community-wide rally at the old Ellis Auditorium to show support for Germany's beleaguered Jews. After the meeting, Maxon received a letter — signed by Dr. Ettelson, Rabbi Cohn, and President Jacob Felsenthal for Children of Israel, and Rabbi Morris Taxon and President Sam Shainberg on behalf of Baron Hirsch — thanking Maxon for his support of the Jewish cause. "To us as Jews," officials of the two congregations wrote, "this spontaneous and fine manifestation of sympathy and brotherliness naturally brought strength and solace in this dark hour of trial and tribulation for Israel."

Felsenthal, whose own ancestors had come to the United States from Germany in the early 1850s, did not live to witness the horrors of Hitler's so-called "final solution" for the Jews of Europe. He died in February 1939 at seventy-three. After Felsenthal's death the congregation's vice president, Abe Wurzburg, took the helm. Wurzburg, the president of his family's packaging business, subsequently was elected by the congregation in his own right and held the leadership until 1945.

On September 1, 1939, Hitler's troops marched into Poland, unleashing the horror that would come to be known as World War II. With newspaper headlines screaming "GERMANY INVADES POLAND" and then, just a few weeks later, "WARSAW FALLS," the members of Children of Israel gathered to observe the High Holy Days in greater numbers than ever before.

ABE WURZBURG
Congregation President, 1939-1945

To accommodate the overflow crowd, the congregation for the first time held two services simultaneously on the eve of Rosh Hashanah and Yom Kippur, one in the sanctuary and one in the vestry, a meeting room in the basement often used by the Junior Congregation. (The custom of having two consecutive services in the sanctuary on the High Holy Days was established later, in 1947.)

During the war years, there were two milestone occasions in the life of the congregation: in 1943 the members changed Children of Israel's name to Temple Israel, and a year later they observed Temple Israel's ninetieth anniversary. Merrill Kremer chaired the anniversary celebration in April 1944, a somewhat scaled-down affair due to the war. Hattie Brooks, the person who had been a member for the longest time, was honored on the occasion, and as a measure of the growing recognition of the role of women in religious, cultural, and community affairs, four women's organizations participated in the services: the Sisterhood; Salon Circle, the oldest Jewish women's cultural group in Memphis; the Regina Lodge of the United Order of True Sisters; and the local section of the National Council of Jewish Women. All four groups had been organized by Temple members.

Under Wurzburg's leadership, the congregation amended its bylaws to provide for representatives of the Brotherhood and the Junior Congregation to sit on the Board, and it created two new honorary titles to pay tribute to two longtime officers. Benjamin Goodman, Sr., who had helped the congregation with numerous financial matters in his many years as treasurer, was named honorary treasurer. (In 1985, his son, Benjamin Goodman, Jr., would be named an honorary trustee.) And Maurice Joseph, who had succeeded Jacob Goldsmith as warden, was named honorary warden. By and large,

however, congregational activities and even Board meetings during this period were dominated by the country's all-out effort to defeat Germany and Japan. So pervasive was the war effort that shortly after the attack on Pearl Harbor, Wurzburg established a War Activities Committee, with Louis Barnett as its chairman.

As was the case all across the nation, virtually everyone at Temple Israel pitched in to help support the troops and win the war. Early on, war bonds became the patriotic investment of choice; the Board of Trustees used the congregation's cash assets to buy them, and the Temple-sponsored Boy Scout troop did an excellent job of selling them. The scouts, given a war bond sales quota of $225 in 1944, went out and sold a whopping $40,000 in war bonds. The following year, under the leadership of Scoutmaster I.G. Goldsmith, the troop surpassed its own record, chalking up more than $70,000 in war bond sales to win a citywide contest.

In 1944 M.A. Lightman, Sr., and Aaron Scharff, Sr., then president and vice-president, respectively, of the local Jewish Welfare Fund, also served as vice chairmen of the Memphis and Shelby County War

Troop 25 received this citation from the Treasury Department in 1944.

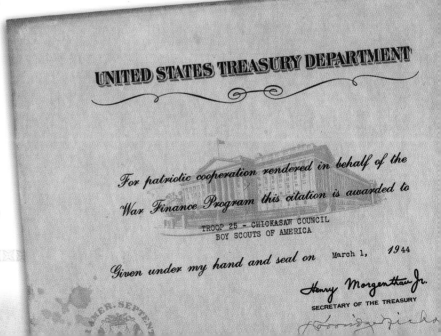

UNITED STATES TREASURY DEPARTMENT

For patriotic cooperation rendered in behalf of the War Finance Program this citation is awarded to

TROOP 25 — CHICKASAW COUNCIL
BOY SCOUTS OF AMERICA

Given under my hand and seal on March 1, 1944

Henry Morgenthau Jr.
SECRETARY OF THE TREASURY

and Welfare Fund Campaign, the wartime version of Shelby United Neighbors (a forerunner of United Way). The drive raised more than $1.1 million to support twenty-two agencies, including the War Prisoners' Aid, the U.S.O., and the United Seamen's Service. Meanwhile, the Sisterhood opened a canteen at Temple, where the ladies served free meals every Sunday evening to servicemen of all faiths. By November 1944 they had served sixteen thousand meals to Armed Forces personnel stationed in and around Memphis.[67]

Approximately four hundred members of the

Meals on Wheels: In the late 1940s, the congregation purchased a rolling cart, enabling Sisterhood volunteers (LEFT TO RIGHT) Sylvia Greif, Betty Dlugach, and Dorothy Davis to serve three dozen dinners at a time.

Temple Israel family served in the Armed Forces during World War II, many of them overseas. Even the rabbis went to war. Rabbi Dudley Weinberg, who had succeeded Morton Cohn as the assistant rabbi, entered the Armed Forces as a chaplain in 1943, and Weinberg's successor, Rabbi Leo Stillpass, followed suit in 1944. That same year the congregation launched a publication called *The Duffel Bag*, which was mailed to all Temple members in military service, as well as to their families. The first issue contained a dispatch from Rabbi Weinberg — by then, Captain Weinberg — who already had a year's service as a military chaplain under his belt. "I've discovered much about religion and the things a man really cares about that I didn't know before and probably would never have learned in the civilian rabbinate," Weinberg wrote from his base on an island in the Pacific. "I celebrated Pesach in the jungle wilderness with more men than I've ever seen in one Temple on Yom Kippur, and with a lot more of the kind of religion that counts."

Each issue of *The Duffel Bag* carried dozens of newsy tidbits about members of the congregation who were on active duty. One item, headlined "Youngest

Major We Know," spread the word that "Leslie Gruber, 24 years old, has just been promoted to the rank of Major." Another, that "Captain Edgar Haas, Jr., was awarded the Distinguished Flying Cross." Readers of *The Duffel Bag* found out where the boys — and a few girls — from Temple were stationed ("Lt. Elias Goldsmith, Jr., has moved to the Philippines after eight months in New Guinea . . . . He has written that it is a fairyland by comparison to his recent station — but only by comparison"); they discovered who had recently enlisted or been drafted into military service ("Alvin Salomon, Ernie Lee and David Hiller took a trip to Ft. Oglethorpe and are now Privates in Uncle Sam's employ"); and they got word of wartime marriages ("Jocelyn Plough and Lt. [j.g.] William Rudner were married July 27 at Miami Beach, where William, having

returned from the South Pacific, is an instructor at the Sub-Chaser Training School"). It was in *The Duffel Bag* that bad news (April 1945: "Pvt. Jack H. Dlugach Missing in Action") and good news (June 1945: "Jack Dlugach Safe") was relayed around the world to soldiers, sailors, and marines who were far away from home. "Wherever you may be," Dudley Weinberg wrote in *The Duffel Bag* to Temple Israel's men in the Armed Forces, "I pray that you are safe and well. Let's stay on the ball and get this vile thing over with. We've all got a lot to go home to."

Sadly, not everyone did make it home. Fourteen young men from Temple Israel lost their lives in World War II: Edward M. Allenberg, Peter O. Binswanger, Harry H. Cohn, Milton H. Levitch, Benjamin H. Levy, Jr., Sherman M. Levy, Leo Malkin, Edgar M. Rothschild, Jr.,

In reverent tribute to the dauntless courage, the unfaltering devotion, the patriotic loyalty of those of our congregational family who gave their all to country and humanity in World War II

Lovingly dedicated by the Sisterhood of Temple Israel, Memphis, Tennessee

Edward M. Allenberg
Peter O. Binswanger
Harry H. Cohn
Milton H. Levitch
Benjamin H. Levy, Jr.
Sherman M. Levy
Leo Malkin
Edgar M. Rothschild, Jr.
David Lester Smith
David H. Steppach, Jr.
Joseph M. Sugarman, Jr.
Norman Summerfield, Jr.
Erwin Weis
Bernard Yolles

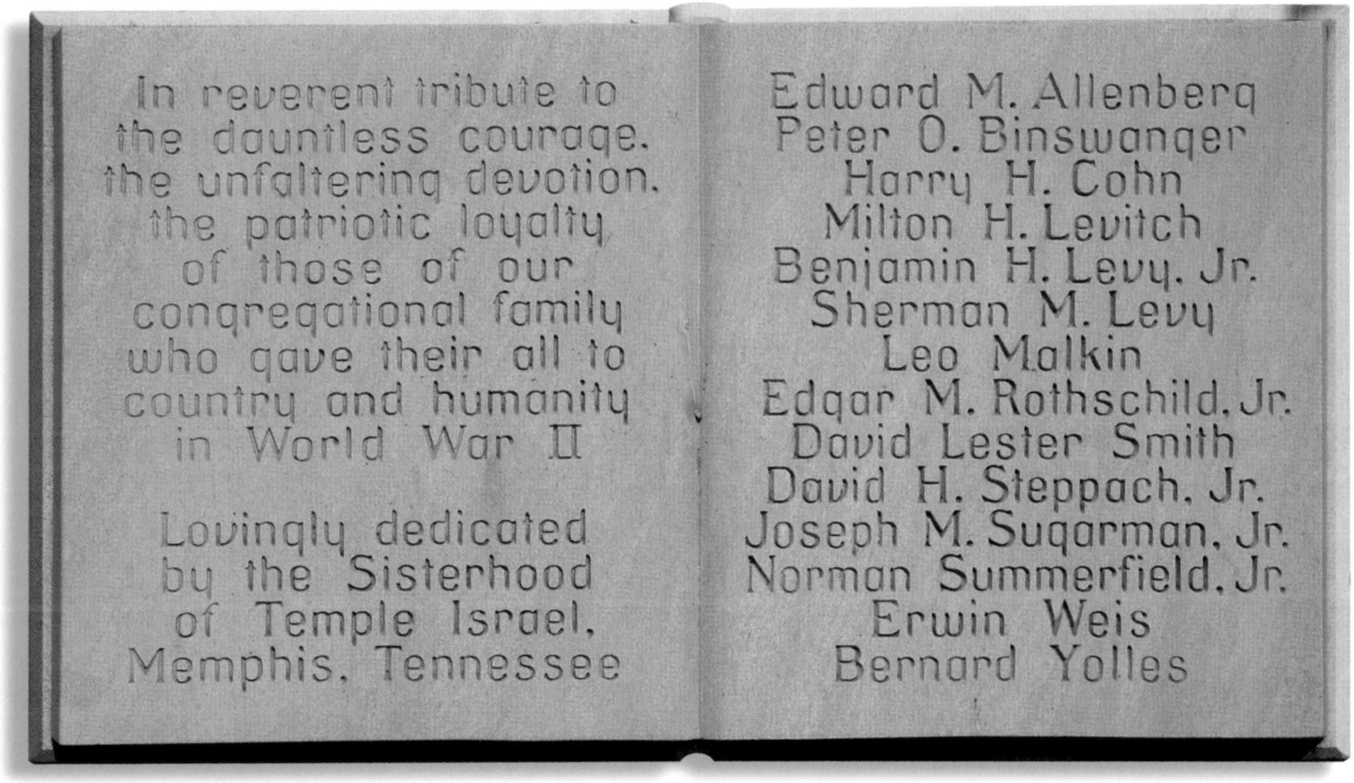

David Lester Smith, David H. Steppach, Jr., Joseph M. Sugarman, Jr., Norman Summerfield, Jr., Erwin Weis, and Bernard Yolles. Their names are inscribed on a War Memorial at the Temple cemetery that was donated by the Sisterhood and dedicated on June 1, 1947.

Though he was not a member of the congregation, the death of James Maxon in the war also caused great sadness at Temple Israel. Maxon, who had joined the Canadian Royal Air Force even before the United States was drawn into the war, was the son of Episcopal Bishop James M. Maxon, the organizer of the post-*Kristallnacht* rally in 1938 that had so heartened the local Jewish community. Upon hearing of the younger Maxon's death, the Temple Board wired its condolences to his parents and made a donation to the British War Relief Fund in his memory.

Despite their wartime losses, the members of Temple Israel gathered for their annual meeting in December 1945 in an atmosphere of gratitude and thanksgiving. The war was over, most of the boys had, in fact, come home, and everyone was looking forward to getting back to normal. Five hundred members of the congregational family turned out for the dinner meeting, a festive affair held in the Continental Ballroom at The Peabody. When the time came to elect new officers, attorney Leo Bearman, Sr., was chosen to succeed Abe Wurzburg as president.

Bearman's first order of business was to hire a new assistant rabbi for the congregation. He appointed former President Abe Wurzburg to chair a search committee, comprised of Louis Barnett, William Loewenberg, Marx Borod, G.D. Strauss, Charles

LEO BEARMAN, SR.
Congregation President, 1945-1951

Goodman, Abe Plough, and Elias Goldsmith, Sr. Their work culminated on April 8, 1946, with the hiring of a young rabbi by the name of James Aaron Wax, then the assistant rabbi at United Hebrew Congregation in St. Louis. Wax started work at Temple Israel that July and was promoted to associate rabbi the following year, with the understanding that he would become senior rabbi when Ettelson retired.

At the outset, Wax was responsible for supervising the religious school and developing adult education courses, but it was not long before he also took on the task of writing the congregation's newsletter, *The Voice*. His new, four-page version of *The Voice* was so well received it soon became a weekly, rather than a bi-weekly, publication.

Around this time the congregation lost two of its oldest and most active members. The first was Isidore Dinkelspiel, who had arrived in Memphis in 1897 from Bavaria (by way of Cincinnati, Atlanta, and Pine Bluff, Arkansas) and served for decades as the congregation's financial secretary, handling an array of administrative and record-keeping chores. To fill the void left by Dinkelspiel's death in 1947, Temple Israel hired its first professional executive secretary, Justin Rothman. The following year, the congregation's honorary president, Hardwig Peres, passed away at the age of ninety.

Meanwhile, the congregation was experiencing its own version of the nation's post-war baby boom. As young men returned from military service, got married, and started families, the membership of Temple Israel grew from 914 families in 1944 to 1,043 families in 1948, to more than

1,100 families by the end of 1949. The influx left the religious school, where the enrollment jumped 40 percent from 1947 to 1949, bursting at the seams. There was only one thing to do. At the annual meeting in 1947, President Bearman announced the launch of a $300,000 capital campaign to build a new school building, and three years later, on a Sunday morning in June 1950, the congregation broke ground for the

new facility. Eight-year-old Bobye Goodman, whose father, Charles Goodman, had chaired the fund-raising campaign, was given the honor of turning the first shovel-full of dirt. A year and a half later the fine new school building, featuring twenty-two classrooms, a library, and offices, was completed.

At the same time the congregation made a number of improvements to the main Temple building. At the

Bobye Goodman breaking ground for a new religious school building in 1950, under the watchful eyes of (**LEFT TO RIGHT**) *President Leo Bearman, Sr., Past President Abe Wurzburg, Honorary President Louis Barnett, Rabbi Harry W. Ettelson, Confirmation Class President Ellen Schiffman, Rabbi James Wax, Junior Congregation President Robert Kline, Parent-Teachers Association President Dorothy Klein, Brotherhood President Herschel Feibelman, and Sisterhood Vice President Lenore Binswanger.*

urging of Mildred Haas, who pointed out with dismay that the architects had failed to include kitchen facilities in the new building, the Board approved an expenditure of more than $23,000 to update the existing kitchen. In addition, after much discussion and many delays — and persistent lobbying by William Loewenberg, Abe Lewis, and others — the Board allocated money to provide air conditioning for the auditorium and the vestry. (The costly job of installing air conditioning in the sanctuary was not undertaken until 1953.)

While all this was going on, a number of issues arose that confronted the Board of Trustees with a dilemma: did they have the right on behalf of the

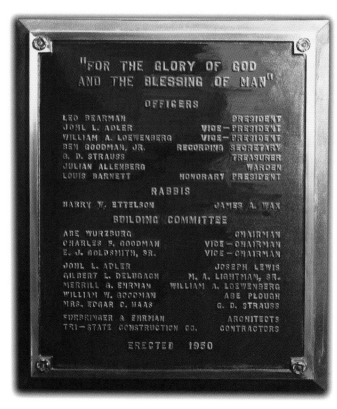

The plaque commemorating the construction of the new religious school building in 1950.

congregation to endorse a cause, or take a stand, that was essentially political in nature? One of the first times this question came up was in September 1949, after the Central Conference of American Rabbis (CCAR) adopted a resolution urging Congress to enact into law President Harry Truman's proposal for a system of compulsory national health insurance. Dr. Morton J. Tendler, representing a group of members known as the Temple Israel Physicians' Group, wrote to the Board asking if the congregation was officially going to support the CCAR's action. In response, the Board passed a motion that night that not only resolved the immediate problem, but also guided the trustees' decisions for many years to come whenever thorny political issues threatened to disturb the equilibrium of the congregation.

The resolution began by asserting, "The rabbis of Temple, as individuals and not as representatives of Temple or its membership, have the right to express themselves, either individually or in concert with other rabbis, on any public question, as indeed is their obligation in furtherance of a program of social justice, the achievement of which is a goal of Judaism." It went on to say, however, that "no expression of opinion by the rabbis of the Temple . . . is in any manner an expression of an organized opinion of the Temple, or of any of its members, the rabbis not being representatives either of the Temple or its members in such matters. The Board of Temple Israel reaffirms the religious character of the Temple," the resolution concluded, "which is not a proper forum for political discussion."

As strange as it may seem to later generations of Reform Jews, no political issue from the 1930s through the 1950s was more problematic for the congregation and its rabbis — indeed, for the entire Reform Movement — than Zionism. At its outset, the

Reform Movement had been totally opposed to Zionism. "We consider ourselves no longer a nation, but a religious community," the founders of American Reform Judaism had stated emphatically in the Pittsburgh Platform, adopted in 1885, "and therefore expect neither a return to Palestine . . . nor the restoration of any of the laws concerning the Jewish state." As a practical matter, the early Reform Jews feared that supporting a Jewish state in Palestine might cause others to question their loyalty to America, where Jews had found a new Promised Land that offered not only religious and political freedom, but also unlimited economic opportunity. And philosophically, they felt that political Zionism would compromise what they saw as the universal spirit of Judaism, the prophetic mission of Jews to bring peace and justice to the world. Thus when Theodor Herzl convened the First World Zionist Congress in 1897, the Central Conference of American Rabbis adopted a resolution that said unequivocally, "We totally disapprove of any attempt for the establishment of a Jewish state."[68]

As the times changed, however, so did the Reform attitude toward Zionism. In the 1930s, when the Jews of Europe grew desperate for somewhere — *anywhere* — to go, the Reform Movement dropped its opposition to a Jewish state and began to support the idea instead. "The time has now come," the Union of American Hebrew Congregations resolved in 1937, "for all Jews, irrespective of ideological differences, to unite in the activities leading to the establishment of a Jewish homeland in Palestine, and we urge our constituency to give their financial and moral support to the work of rebuilding Palestine."[69]

While some of the nation's Reform rabbis — Abba Hillel Silver and Stephen Wise, for example — spoke out passionately in support of a Jewish state, others, including Louis Wolsey, Morris Lazaron, and Temple

Israel's own former spiritual leader, William Fineshriber, remained just as passionately opposed to the idea. In 1942, after the members of the Central Conference of American Rabbis voted to support the formation of a Jewish army in Palestine, Wolsey, Lazaron, and Fineshriber, along with about eighty-five other rabbis and lay people, formed an anti-Zionist organization called the American Council for Judaism. At its peak, the Council had a number of local chapters, as well as regional offices in Chicago, Dallas, San Francisco, and Richmond, Virginia, but after the State of Israel became a reality in 1948, the organization lost its momentum. Eventually even Louis Wolsey resigned.

Temple Israel's members, like their counterparts in Reform congregations all across the nation, were divided on the issue of Zionism. The congregation's former president, Dr. Louis Levy, was a fervent Zionist, as was its honorary president, Hardwig Peres; indeed, Peres' name was virtually synonymous with the Zionist Movement in Memphis. Along with Levy and Peres, the official letterhead of the Memphis Zionist District in 1948 listed two other Temple members among its directors — Abe D. Waldauer and Ernest Adler.[70] At the other end of the spectrum, former Temple President Milton Binswanger, Sr., and others strongly supported the American Council for Judaism. The majority of Temple members, having been schooled in the beliefs of Classical Reform, adopted an ambivalent position that could best be described as non-Zionist.

The same could be said of the congregation's rabbis. Ettelson, who had declined to join the American Council for Judaism, also declined to lend his official support to pro-Zionist groups. Unofficially, however, there is some evidence that he was not as opposed to them as his congregation might have believed. In June 1943, Ettelson had an interesting exchange of letters with Mortimer May of Nashville, who had called on the rabbi on behalf of the Zionist cause. "I would take advantage of this opportunity to extend to you my appreciation for your most cordial offer to be of cooperation, in every way possible, with the work of the Memphis Zionist District," May wrote to Ettelson after they met. "I left Memphis very much encouraged about the general Zionist picture and felt that the community was, like so many others in the region, working in full harmony for this great project of our people."[71] A few weeks later Ettelson replied, "You envisaged a program in which every Jew, it seems to me, should find it possible to participate materially and morally. I hope to be able to take a more active share in some of the actual work here, even while having certain reservations ideologically, though not idealistically and realistically."[72]

Whatever Ettelson's true feelings were about a Jewish homeland in Palestine, they did not outweigh his desire to keep peace in the congregation. Thus, when Rabbi Arthur Lelyveld wrote to Ettelson from New York in April 1945 to ask if Ettelson would arrange for him to speak to a group of Temple members on behalf of an organization called the Committee on Unity for Palestine, Ettelson replied, "I cannot sponsor the meeting officially." On the question of Zionism, he explained, "We in the Congregation . . . have maintained the attitude that our members shall follow their own convictions and have been fortunate so far in maintaining congregational *esprit de corps*." Still, Ettelson did not turn Lelyveld down flat; he put him in touch with Hardwig Peres, "a warm friend of mine, and an ardent Zionist," for help in organizing the meeting.[73]

Not surprisingly, the Board, too, declined to make waves over the issue of Zionism. In 1951, when the congregation was asked by the state manager of Bonds for Israel to participate in the Israel Bonds campaign, the Board passed a motion that said, "It is not the policy of our congregation to participate, as a congregation, in any fund-raising campaign." Still, Ben Goodman, Jr., who made the motion, was quick to add that it "should not be construed as a disapproval of the aims and purposes of the project, the furtherance of which is merely being left to the discretion of the individual members."

Quite a few Temple members supported Israel Bond drives during the 1950s, and in 1957 S.L. Kopald, Jr., then vice president of Temple Israel, served as chairman of the citywide Israel Bonds campaign. But not until 1972 would Temple Israel sponsor, under the chairmanship of Herschel Feibelman, an Israel Bond dinner of its own. Interestingly, the honoree on that occasion was none other than Dr. Harry W. Ettelson.

Campaign Chairman S.L. Kopald, Jr., applauding Eleanor Roosevelt following her speech at a Bonds for Israel dinner at Baron Hirsch Synagogue in 1957. In the background is Sarah Belz.

Rabbis James Wax and Harry W. Ettelson with Herschel Feibelman at Temple Israel's first Israel Bonds dinner in 1972.

Ultimately, just as there had been room in the past for disagreement on other issues, there was room at Temple Israel in the middle of the twentieth century for disagreement on Zionism. Meanwhile, as the congregation neared the end of its first century, its members were in harmony on most other questions of religious outlook and purpose.

In November 1951 the members of Temple elected a new president, William Loewenberg, an entrepreneur who had interests in more than half a dozen businesses, including Southern Leather, Mills Morris, Perkins Oil Co., and Air-Temp. At the same time, they also paved the way for a change in rabbinic leadership. Upon Ettelson's announcement that he intended to retire during the congregation's centennial year, the members unanimously elected James A. Wax, who had been Ettelson's heir apparent since 1946, to be his successor.

So it was that in 1953-54, Temple Israel marked not only its hundredth birthday, but also two other historic occasions: Harry W. Ettelson's retirement and James A. Wax's installation as senior rabbi. Under the overall chairmanship of former President

Leo Bearman, Sr., with Benjamin Goodman, Sr., and Mildred Haas serving as co-chairs, the congregation celebrated with a full calendar of centennial events stretching from October to April.

First on the schedule was a special Friday night service in October 1953 in honor of Ettelson's seventieth birthday. The following month Temple hosted a convention of the Kentucky-Tennessee Federation of Reform Congregations, Sisterhoods, and Brotherhoods, as well as an all-day institute for Christian clergy, religious school teachers, and theological students in the Mid-South. Next came the centennial year annual meeting, during which the eight hundred congregants in attendance voted to name the Temple's auditorium in honor of Ettelson. After the speeches and formalities, including an address by Dr. William Fineshriber, the members were treated to a skit called "100 Years in Review." Written by Beatrice Stern and produced by Paul S. Schwartz, the skit featured Sam A. Myar, Jr.; Hilda Magdovitz; her son, Earl Magdovitz; Jack Lieberman; and Hallie Rubin.

WILLIAM LOEWENBERG
Congregation President, 1951-1954

In February the congregation honored Dr. Ettelson at yet another Friday night service, this time to mark his retirement. (Though Ettelson and his wife, Nell, later moved back to Philadelphia, their ties to Memphis, and especially to Temple Israel, remained strong. Every year until his death in 1975,

Ettelson sent a hand-written message of congratulations to the congregation to be read aloud at the annual meeting.)

A centennial banquet was held at The Peabody on March 2, 1954, exactly a hundred years after the congregation received its charter from the Tennessee Legislature. Tennessee Governor Frank Clement participated in the program, along with Memphis Mayor Frank Tobey, but the featured attraction was a speech by one of the luminaries of the Reform Movement at the time, Dr. Abba Hillel Silver of Cleveland, Ohio. To mark the occasion, the congregation also published a history of Temple Israel titled

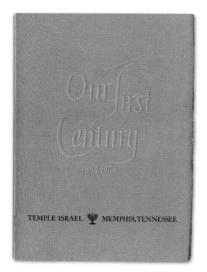

Our First Century, 1854-1954, written by Rabbi James A. Wax and his wife, Helen Goldstrom Wax, and edited by Ernest Lee.

Finally, in April 1954, having spent the previous six months celebrating its past, the congregation turned its attention to the future by formally installing James A. Wax as senior rabbi. Accompanied on the pulpit by Dr. Julian Morgenstern, president emeritus of Hebrew Union College, and his old friend and mentor, Dr. Ferdinand M. Isserman, the rabbi of Temple Israel in St. Louis, Wax officially accepted the responsibilities of his new position and welcomed the opportunity, and the challenge, of leading Temple Israel into its second century.

Temple Israel's Centennial Banquet at The Peabody, March 2, 1954

If there was any doubt among the members of Temple Israel about what the focus of James Wax's rabbinate would be, all they had to do was think back...

. . . to the sermon he delivered on the eve of Rosh Hashanah in September 1946, when he was the congregation's newly-arrived assistant rabbi. Wax's speech that night was not the kind of cautious, predictable discourse a young rabbi might be expected to give on his first High Holy Days at a new congregation. On the contrary, it was a stirring call to action.

"Social justice, the genuine concern for one's fellow man, is the cornerstone of Judaism and it must become the cornerstone upon which the world is built," Wax declared, speaking in a deep, resonant voice that still echoed in the memories of his congregants many years after he was gone. "Too many of us appease our conscience by giving to charity, forgetting that, as Maimonides said, 'Greater than giving to charity is to remove the need of it.' In Judaism, charity is the last resort and justice is the first requirement.

"Religion is not what some would make it, 'a Sabbath asset and a weekday liability,'" Wax continued. "A religion that emphasizes righteousness and not ritual; that emphasizes conduct and not creed; that emphasizes deed and not dogma offers the solution to the problems that confront us. Religion confined to sanctuary walls, religion on a part-time basis can do little; but religion whose voice is heard everywhere and whose influence is constantly felt will

JAMES A. WAX
Spiritual Leader of Temple Israel, 1954-1978

steer mankind from confusion to certainty, from strife to security. The idealism of Israel's prophets must be heard and heeded in the market place and in the legislative assembly, in the industrial conference and in the peace parley. Let not the voice of religion be muffled, its spirit stifled and its influence ignored. Let us learn the meaning of morality and make it meaningful in our daily lives and labors."[74]

Born in 1912, Wax had grown up in the small town of Herculaneum, Missouri, where his father, Morris, an immigrant from Russia, operated a dry goods store, served on the school board, and was active in Democratic politics. An excellent student and champion debater, the young Wax — Jimmy to his friends — had thought he might become a lawyer until he went to St. Louis for the High Holy Days in 1929 (there was no synagogue in Herculaneum) and heard Rabbi Ferdinand Isserman give a sermon about social justice and human dignity. The experience altered the course of his life. After graduating from Southeast Missouri State College, Wax enrolled at Hebrew Union College in Cincinnati, where he was ordained in 1941. Before coming to Memphis in 1946, he served as the assistant rabbi at the United Hebrew Congregation in St. Louis and as the interim rabbi at the North Shore Congregation Israel in Glencoe, Illinois. It was while he was in Glencoe that he met and married Helen Goldstrom, who was the acting director of the National Federation of Temple Youth at the time.

From the beginning of his tenure at Temple Israel, Wax practiced the "social action" that he preached. Early on, seeing the need for improved care of the mentally ill, he helped found the agency that became the Memphis-Shelby County Mental Health Association, and he served on the state's first Mental Health Commission. As time went on he worked with the Governor's Committee for Employment of the Physically Handicapped, the National Conference of Christians and Jews (later called the National Conference of Community and Justice), Memphis Planned Parenthood, the Mid-South Medical Center Board, the Memphis Urban League, and many other groups trying to solve social welfare and community relations problems. Distressed by the racial discrimination he found in Memphis, where virtually all public facilities — schools, restrooms, restaurants, buses, swimming pools, movie theaters, and even libraries — were segregated, he was determined to help promote change. On one occasion, when he learned that a local charitable organization was having trouble finding a place to hold a racially integrated meeting, Wax invited the group to meet at Temple. His philosophy, as he later explained to writer Joan Beifuss, was simple: "Religion should transform the environment, not capitulate to it."[75]

It was not surprising, therefore, that when the biracial Memphis Committee on Community Relations (MCCR) was formed in 1958, Wax was one of the community leaders chosen to serve on it. Organized in the aftermath of the violence that had erupted in Little Rock over the desegregation of its Central High School, the MCCR worked behind the scenes during the late 1950s and early '60s to negotiate and implement the peaceful desegregation of most of Memphis's public facilities (except the schools, which were desegregated in 1973 by court order).

Wax was not the only member of the Temple family who worked to promote civil rights during this period. A number of congregants also became advocates for change, notably attorney Herschel Feibelman, who served as chairman of the city's War on Poverty Committee from 1966-69; Jack Goldsmith, president of Goldsmith's department stores, and Mel Grinspan, an executive with the Shainberg stores, who worked together quietly to encourage downtown retailers to hire black salespeople; Marvin Ratner, who gave up a partnership in the prominent law firm of Heiskell Donelson to form, along with two other white attorneys and two black attorneys, the city's first integrated law firm; and Jocelyn Wurzburg, who founded the Memphis Panel of American Women in an effort to promote interracial and interfaith dialogue. When Myra Dreifus discovered that thousands of the city's schoolchildren from low-income families were going without lunch each day, she recruited a biracial group of women, including many Temple members, to join her in forming what came to be known as the Fund for Needy School Children. The group raised money from churches and synagogues to provide school lunches for hungry children, persuaded the Shelby County Quarterly Court to levy a special tax for that purpose, and later, after federal funds became available to meet the need, expanded to provide numerous other services in the public schools.[76]

Still, the congregation was, in general, wary of sticking its neck out on the issue of civil rights, especially after The Temple in Atlanta was bombed in 1958 by what was suspected to be a Klan-like group of white racists. Wax repeatedly spoke out in favor of integration during this period, but in contrast to some of his rabbinical colleagues, he did not participate in protest marches. As a civil rights activist he was much more comfortable working quietly, behind the scenes, through organizations like the Memphis Committee on Community Relations and the Memphis Ministers Association. "He never wanted to be, as he used to say, 'a general without an army,'" his wife, Helen, explained many years later. "He never wanted to put Temple Israel out in front by itself."

Thus it was not as the rabbi of Temple Israel, but as the president of the Memphis Ministers Association, that James A. Wax stood at the forefront of one of the most dramatic protest marches in the city's history — the solemn procession of black and white ministers who made their way from St. Mary's Episcopal Cathedral to Mayor Henry Loeb's office in City Hall on Friday, April 5, 1968, the day after Dr. Martin Luther King, Jr., was killed in Memphis by a sniper's bullet.

King had come to Memphis in support of the sanitation workers, whose strike against the city had dragged on since February of that year, growing more bitter by the day. By April the two sides were still at a stalemate: the workers were seeking a small pay raise and, more importantly, recognition by the city of their union, the American Federation of State, County, and Municipal Employees; the city, led by Mayor Henry Loeb, kept insisting that it could not — and would not — negotiate with the workers because the strike violated city and state laws and was, therefore, illegal.

As racial tensions in Memphis mounted, Wax and others had tried in vain to mediate the dispute. Abe Plough, certain that the turmoil was going to have dire consequences for the city, had called on the mayor with an offer to fund the workers' pay raises personally if that would lead to a settlement; Loeb, intent on breaking the strike, declined the offer.[77] Wax, for his part, had brought Loeb and the union leaders together for a face-to-face meeting at St. Mary's Cathedral on the evening of February 18. The discussions dragged on until five o'clock in the morning, but during all that time Loeb steadfastly refused to speak directly to the national union representatives, and the weary participants finally adjourned with no compromise in sight.[78] Ironically, Henry Loeb was a former member of Wax's congregation who had dropped out and joined the Episcopal Church. Still, he and Wax had maintained a cordial relationship; Loeb had even invited Wax to give the invocation at his inauguration.

Their cordial relationship notwithstanding, James Wax was frustrated and furious when he and other religious leaders crowded into the mayor's office on the day after King was murdered. In a characteristic gesture, one that punctuated his speech whenever he felt strongly about a subject, Wax shook his index finger at Loeb and said, "We come here with a great deal of sadness and, frankly, a great deal of anger. What happened in this city is a result of oppression and injustice, the inhumanity of man to man; and we have come to you for leadership in ending the situation. There are laws far greater than the laws of Memphis and Tennessee, and these are the laws of God. We fervently ask you not to hide any longer behind legal technicalities and slogans, but to speak out at last in favor of human dignity."[79]

April 5, 1968: In the aftermath of the King assassination, Rabbi James Wax urges Mayor Henry Loeb (back to camera) to "speak out at last in favor of human dignity."

Later that day, at Temple Israel's Friday evening worship service, Wax's emotions boiled over again in his sermon, a heartfelt eulogy for King that he delivered, with great feeling, in place of the speech he had planned to give that night. "Some people said, 'Isn't it too bad it happened here?'" Wax noted, speaking of King's assassination. "No, my friends. I love this city, but this doesn't disturb me so much. I am disturbed by the conditions of racial injustice that prevail here. I am concerned about the bigotry and prejudice in our community. *This* disturbs me." Nevertheless, in words reminiscent of Lincoln's Gettysburg Address, Wax went on to assure his congregation that Martin Luther King did not die in vain. "This city shall witness a new spirit and the memory of this great prophet of our time shall be honored," the rabbi predicted. "There will be the bigots and the segregationists and the so-called respectable but unrighteous people who will resist. But in the scheme of history, God's will does prevail."[80]

In the aftermath of his confrontation with Henry Loeb, which was captured by television cameras and prominently featured on local and national news programs that night, Wax received bundles of hate mail. He even heard from a few members of his own congregation who, as Helen Wax recalled, "thought he should have kept his mouth shut." Loeb, on the other hand, apparently took it all in stride. Three years later, when Wax was celebrating his twenty-fifth anniversary with Temple Israel, Loeb was among those who sent the rabbi a message of congratulations. "Both of us have seen a lot of things happen in Memphis in [the last] quarter-century, with a lot of progress and occasional setbacks," the mayor wrote, glossing over the terrible events of 1968, "but withal, we both have had the best interests of the City at heart at all times, in our own way."[81]

To many Memphians, Wax's expression of righteous indignation on April 5, 1968, stood out as one of the few bright spots in a very bleak time in the city's history. "I don't imagine there is anything in Rabbi Wax's life that stands taller than what he did during the garbage strike," Dr. Harry E. Moore, regional director of the National Conference of Christians and Jews, told *The Commercial Appeal* at the time of Wax's death in 1989.[82] Indeed, in the eyes of many of his admirers — though not necessarily in the eyes of the rabbi, himself — it was James A. Wax's finest hour.

While community service and civil rights advocacy would always play a huge role in Wax's life, he spent most of his time, like other rabbis, keeping up with the day-to-day responsibilities of shepherding his own flock. Out of respect to Ettelson, under whom he had served for eight years, Wax made few immediate changes when he became senior rabbi in 1954. The congregation was still Classical Reform in its religious outlook and practices, and to a large extent, Wax preferred to keep it that way. Still, with regard to certain rituals, Wax preferred doing things the old-fashioned way. One of the first changes he did make was to arrange for a genuine shofar to be blown during Rosh Hashanah services; at some point in the past, it seems, Temple Israel had substituted a *faux* shofar — that is, a trumpet — for the traditional ram's horn.

Another religious custom that had fallen out of favor with the congregation, the bar mitzvah ceremony, also began to reappear during the 1950s. Thirteen-year-old Henry Levy, who was born in Nazi Germany in November 1938, six days after the terror and turmoil of *Kristallnacht*, was among the first in modern times to celebrate this rite of passage at Temple Israel; at the request of his

A shofar from the Adler Collection

family, he became a bar mitzvah in 1951 after taking private lessons from Wax, then the associate rabbi. Twin brothers Phil and Arnold Weinstein had a joint bar mitzvah ceremony at Temple in 1953, and Henry Levy's cousins, Joe Levy and Larry Adler, followed suit in 1954 and 1955, respectively. Still, bar mitzvahs would continue to be the exception, rather than the rule, at Temple for another fifteen or twenty years, and it would be 1971 before the first girl at Temple, Gwyn Felt, would celebrate a bat mitzvah. Gradually, however, the traditional ceremony began to grow in popularity. By 1960 there were eighteen children enrolled in Temple Israel's mid-week Hebrew classes, seven of whom were candidates for bar mitzvah.

Temple Israel had a membership of about twelve hundred families when Wax became senior rabbi in 1954, and more than six hundred children were enrolled in its religious school. Due to the post-war baby boom, the student population was still growing rapidly — so rapidly that in 1955, just four years after the new school building was completed, the congregation found it necessary to construct two additional classrooms on the balcony of the Ettelson Auditorium.

Much of the adult education at the time was conducted under the auspices of the Temple Brotherhood, which in 1955 was named "Outstanding Brotherhood in the United States" among those with fewer than five hundred members. The Brotherhood also sponsored the congregation's annual interfaith Thanksgiving service and subsidized a baseball team for eight- to ten-year-

Photo by Rod Phillips

THE 1958 TEMPLE ISRAEL PEEWEES, CHAMPIONS OF THE METHODIST LEAGUE

FRONT ROW (LEFT TO RIGHT): *Rick Samelson(2b), Steve Kopald (cf), Alan Bozof (of), Bobby Jacobs (cf), Paul Cooper (of), Steve Bearman (2b), Bill Jacobs (ss), Russell Haas (inf), David Roman (of).* BACK ROW: *Joel Benham (1b), Ricky Cohn (inf), Bill Levy (c), Eddie Green (3b), Johnny Weiss (inf), Richard Haas (inf), Dick Eisenberg (of), Sammy Fink (p), David Rosenberg (of).* STANDING, *Coach Alan Salomon.*

Photo by Murray Riss

Since the 1950s, the Sisterhood's annual sale of Holland bulbs has funded many projects at Temple Israel and beautified the whole city.

olds, coached by Alan Salomon. In 1958, in true inter-faith spirit, Temple Israel's baseball team won the championship of the Methodist Peewee League.

Meanwhile, the Sisterhood continued to fund a wide array of necessities and extras for the congregation. Most of the money the group donated to Temple came from the sale of flower bulbs from Holland, a fund-raising project, launched in the early 1950s, that would continue to be a mainstay of the Sisterhood's activities for many years to come. It was Amy

Allenberg who originally proposed the idea; she had gone to Birmingham, Alabama, to visit her daughter, Betty Goldstein, and heard that the Sisterhood there was engaged in a similar project. In addition to Allenberg, four other women were instrumental in getting the bulb sales up and running: Rana Goodman, Frankie Cooper, Minette Sissman, and Marie Krivcher.

In the beginning, the bulb project was housed in the Temple basement. "The bulbs came from Holland in wooden crates, and there was no one to help us get them open, so we devised our own system," Frankie Cooper recalled, laughing. "We'd put them at the top of the steps leading to the basement, and we'd push them down the stairs, and the crates would break open." Nothing would go to waste, she noted with pride. "People used to fight over those crates, because they used the wood for kindling." Cooper, who had worked as the manager of the Lerner Shops in Memphis for five years, volunteered at the outset to keep track of the project's income and expenses. She would still be reconciling the books — and ordering the bulbs and recruiting the salespeople — more than fifty years later, with the assistance of her daughter, Joyce Graflund, and Joy Bearman, Gloria Felsenthal, and Judy Royal.

It was not long after Wax became senior rabbi that the Conservative synagogue, Beth Sholom, was established in Memphis. Wax, who understood the need for a local congregation that would offer a middle ground between Reform and Orthodoxy, warmly supported the new synagogue and even solicited donations to its building fund from members of his own congregation. In December 1956, when Beth Sholom dedicated its new synagogue at the corner of Mendenhall Road and what was then known as Sanderlin Lane, he presented a pulpit Bible to Beth Sholom as a gift from Temple Israel, cementing a warm relationship between the two congregations. Years later Beth Sholom would return the favor, giving Temple Israel a handsome silver *yad*, or pointer, for use in its new synagogue.

The question of whether Temple Israel itself should construct a new synagogue first arose in 1956, under the administration of Edward Felsenthal, whose father, Jacob, had led the congregation nearly twenty years earlier. The subject was introduced by S.L. Kopald, Jr., then vice president of the congregation, who proposed at a Board meeting in 1956 that Felsenthal should appoint a special committee "to investigate the feasibility and possibility of acquiring property in East Memphis for the eventual expansion and relocation of our Temple facilities." The motion carried.

Thus began the long and arduous process of acquiring a new facility for Temple Israel in East Memphis, an endeavor that would be subject to numerous starts and stops over a period of twenty years before finally coming to fruition in

S.L. KOPALD, JR.
Congregation President, 1957-1961 and 1963-1964

1976. No one at the time, of course, thought it would take that long. The leaders of the congregation simply began, step by step, to plan for an eventual move.

The first step was to find a suitable piece of land. A committee chaired by real estate developer Harry Dermon advised the Board to look for an eight- to ten-acre tract located in an area bounded by the North Carolina and St. Louis Railroad tracks on the north, Park Avenue on the south, Goodlett Road on the west, and Massey Road — a street that was considered way out in the country back in 1957 — on the east. In the fall of 1958, having considered several possible sites, the Board voted to buy fifteen acres on the west side of White Station Road, just north of Sanderlin Lane. A $50,000 gift from retailer Leo Levy was used to help finance the $100,000 purchase.

Meanwhile, Kopald, Felsenthal, and others went to work to try to convince the congregation that a move out East was necessary. Kopald, having studied an analysis of the members' residential patterns, reported to the Board in January 1957 that more than 53 percent of the congregation's in-town members and, significantly, more than 75 percent of the families with children in the religious school now lived east of East Parkway. Many of the younger members, he noted, were already living east of Perkins Road, more than seven miles east of the Temple's location at Poplar and Montgomery. Felsenthal, for his part, presented evidence that the existing Temple, built in 1915-16 to accommodate a membership of about 350 families, was simply inadequate for a congregation more than three times that size. "The Ettelson Auditorium is even now too small for a Confirmation Class reception," he told the members at the annual meeting in November 1957. "We have a major need for a chapel; we are pressed for space in our religious school; and the seats and flooring in our main sanctuary need repair or replacement."

That night Felsenthal retired from office, and the members elected the tall, gentlemanly Kopald — better known as "Kopie" — to succeed him. At the same time they named Louis Barnett honorary president, in recognition of his many years of service to the congregation; he would hold the position until his death in 1962.

Kopald, then executive vice president of HumKo Products (later a division of Kraft), was only thirty-six at the time of his election, but he was already well known for his leadership in both the Jewish and general com-

munities. The same year he became president of Temple Israel he also served as president of the Memphis Rotary Club and chairman of the Bonds for Israel campaign. A year earlier he had chaired the Memphis-Shelby County Community Chest. Kopald held so many leadership positions in the community, in fact, that his friends once jokingly presented him with a "Certificate of Perpetual Congratulations."

Among the challenges that greeted Kopald when he took the helm of the congregation, none was more critical than the need to find more space for the religious school, which was filled to overflowing with 735 students and a 40-member faculty. With a move to East Memphis under consideration, it did not make sense to add on to the religious school at Poplar and Montgomery, so the congregation's leadership proposed a different solution: classes for nursery through third grade would be shifted to Saturday mornings, while the upper grades would continue to meet, as in the past, on Sunday mornings. The reaction was "*very traumatic,*" especially among the members who had children in both age groups, Kopald said later. A small number of congregants were so opposed to the plan that when it was finally implemented in 1959, they set up their own religious school, holding classes for a time in a meeting room at a branch bank located on Perkins Road Extended. Though it lasted only a few years, this alternative religious school gave rise to a memorable story, widely circulated at the time, about Louise Wolf, the six-year-old daughter of Joanne and Herbert Wolf, who was asked one day by the librarian at her elementary school if she

LOUIS BARNETT
Honorary President, 1957-1962

went to Sunday school. "Yes, ma'am," Louise replied politely. "I go to the National Bank of Commerce."

In 1961, with 780 children enrolled in the religious school and another 120 high-schoolers involved in the Junior Congregation, Temple Israel began operating a bus that picked up children at several East Memphis locations and transported them to Temple. Since Baron Hirsch Congregation, then located at Vollintine and Evergreen, used some of the same pick-up points for its own religious school bus, a certain amount of confusion was inevitable. "One Sunday I'd get a call from Baron Hirsch telling me one of our kids wound up over there," Herschel Feibelman, then chairman of Temple's Religious School Committee, recalled with a chuckle. "The next Sunday we'd count heads when the kids got off the bus and discover we had one of theirs."

HERBERT KOHN
Congregation President, 1961-1963

Bowing to parents' requests, the Religious School Committee arranged for the mid-week Hebrew classes, as well as the children's choir rehearsals, to meet at Beth Sholom. The arrangement was not entirely satisfactory, Feibelman told the Temple Board, but it was "the only practical solution to the geographical problem."

In spite of the "geographical problem," not everyone was convinced the congregation was ready to take on the expense of building a new Temple. Not least among the doubters was Abe Plough, whose financial support would be critical to the project's success. "It looks like to me not only you, but those that surround you have the impatience of youth, as I can't help but feel you are butting your head against a brick wall," Plough, then sixty-nine, wrote to Kopald, nearly thirty years his junior, in June 1960. "You are completely overlooking the fact that you could not build the kind of Temple and improvements you are talking about for less than $2 million," Plough continued, "and unless you get 70% or $1,400,000 in cash or bankable commitments, it would be a mistake to start." Plough challenged Kopald to go out and try to raise the $1.4 million within twelve months but predicted it would be impossible — in which case, Plough wrote, "you ought to drop the idea, sell the lot [on White Station], raise [a] half million dollars and do what is necessary to the present Temple, as well as any addition." Still, Plough's message was not entirely negative. "I'm sure you understand that it is my desire to be liberal in a donation," he assured Kopald near the end of his frank two-page letter. "You can count me in on either plan . . . ."[83]

As things turned out, Kopald retired from the presidency in 1961 without having launched a fund drive for either the larger or smaller amount. Nevertheless, during the two-year administration of his successor, Malco Theaters executive Herbert Kohn, he continued to keep the goal of a new Temple alive. In January 1963, Kopald appeared before the Executive Committee with a detailed presentation of the need for a new Temple, citing the disadvantages of the existing location and the responsibility of the current members to provide for the future needs of the congregation. In response, the Executive Committee, and later the full Board, unanimously resolved to construct a new Temple on White Station Road at the earliest possible time, and they authorized the president to appoint the necessary committees to get the project underway.

Within a few months Kohn appointed Kopald to chair the overall effort, and the Board authorized the hiring of a professional fund-raiser to conduct a preliminary survey of potential donors. By August 1963 the Architecture Committee, chaired by attorney Ben Goodman, Jr., had hired the local firm of Gassner, Nathan and Browne to begin designing the new facility, in consultation with New York architect Daniel Schwartzman. A new Temple on White Station Road was going to become a reality, it seemed, in the not-too-distant future.

Meanwhile, the congregation and its rabbi continued with their customary activities, along with a few new ones. Among the latter was a trip to Jerusalem that Rabbi Wax and his wife, Helen, took in 1963, together with Kopald and his wife, Mimi, to attend a meeting of the Hebrew Union College Board of Governors, of which both Wax and Kopald were members. With the enthusiastic support of the Board, which granted Wax a leave of absence and defrayed much of the trip's expenses, the Waxes took three additional weeks to tour England and Western Europe, visiting synagogues and other places of Jewish historical interest along the way.

For Wax, whose upbringing in the tiny town of Herculaneum, Missouri, had isolated him from the diversity of Jewish life in large American cities, not to mention from the character of Jewish life in Israel and Europe, the journey was an eye-opener. It is interesting to note that less than a year after he returned from Israel, the Temple Board voted for the first time to purchase State of Israel Bonds, and Wax instituted the practice of reading the Torah as part of Friday night services. Whether or not Wax's visit to Israel and Europe had any direct bearing on these events, one thing seems clear: at a time when America itself was poised on the brink of a cultural revolution, the winds of change were beginning to stir the air, ever so gently, at Temple Israel as well.

By this time ten years had gone by since Wax became Temple Israel's spiritual leader, a decade during which four assistant rabbis — Milton G. Miller, Robert Blinder, Sanford Seltzer, and Sylvin Wolf — had come and gone. When the position of assistant rabbi became vacant again in 1964, Wax made a trip to Hebrew Union College in Cincinnati, where he interviewed six or seven members of the graduating class. For some reason — perhaps because in 1964 not many Reform rabbis wanted to come to the South, where the struggle over civil rights had reached a fever pitch — none of these candidates was hired. Then Wax heard about Harry K. Danziger, a young rabbinical student from Huntington, West Virginia, who had delayed listing his name with the College's Placement Office because he was scheduled to become a chaplain in the Navy after being ordained. The Navy, however, decided it did not require his services, so Danziger was free to make other plans.

At Wax's request, Danziger traveled to Memphis to meet with the Board, and "the consensus prevailed," according to the minutes, "that Mr. Danziger made a very favorable impression." Danziger, for his part, was favorably impressed as well. "One of the first things I saw was the immense deference and respect and friendship between the rabbi and the Board," he said nearly forty years later, thinking back to that Friday night in May 1964 when he visited Temple Israel for the first time. "It was obvious that [Wax] was more than just some kind of professional elected employee . . . I sensed a warm partnership between the lay leaders and the rabbi." The following Monday

MILTON BINSWANGER, JR.
Congregation President, 1964-1966

the Board voted to offer Danziger the position of assistant rabbi, effective July 1, 1964. After taking two days to consider the matter, he accepted.

Danziger, who won the Cora Kahn Award for sermon delivery when he graduated from Hebrew Union College, found plenty of opportunities to put his preaching skills to the test during his first summer at Temple Israel. A week after he arrived, Rabbi Wax entered a local hospital to have surgery for a leg problem, leaving the inexperienced new rabbi to handle anything and everything that came his way. "I did two sermons a week, about eight or nine weddings that were already scheduled, and any funerals that came up," Danziger recalled. "By the time I got to my first Rosh Hashanah, I was not a new, inexperienced rabbi any more." Indeed, by the time the High Holy Days arrived in early September 1964, Danziger had already endeared himself to the congregation, and to one bubbly young congregant, Jeanne Chaban, in particular. After a courtship conducted partly by mail — Jeanne was a sophomore at Washington University in St. Louis that year — the couple became engaged in January 1965 and were married the following August.

In the meantime, the drive for a new Temple was still chugging along. Kopald, who had served another year as president in 1963-64 in order to keep the momentum for a new Temple going, retired from the office again in September 1964. (Two years later he would become chairman of the Board of Governors of Hebrew Union College.) He was succeeded in the Temple presidency by Milton S. Binswanger, Jr., whose father had led the congregation more than three decades earlier. At the same time, Joseph Lewis, who had helped the congregation with numerous business matters as financial secretary and later, as vice president, was named honorary president.

"You are entitled to know," Binswanger told the congregation in his acceptance speech, "that I assume the office of president with the strong conviction that the concept of a new, enlarged, more appropriately situated Temple facility is vital to the growth, even the complete preservation, of Temple Israel, five, ten, or more years into the future." He added, however, "I am interested in seeing it go forward only if you and a large majority of our membership believe . . . that this is vital to the future of Temple Israel."

During the two years of Binswanger's presidency, Executive Director Henry J. Lewis retired, and Joseph Boston, previously of Temple Gates of Prayer in New Orleans, was hired to succeed him; Rabbi Wax was honored on the occasion of his twentieth year with the congregation and twenty-fifth year in the rabbinate; and

JOSEPH LEWIS
Honorary President, 1964-1965

Architectural rendering of the proposed new Temple on White Station Road

Temple Israel contributed $3,100 to the Camp Association for Southern Temples to help with the purchase of a camp site near Utica, Mississippi. (Temple's financial commitment to the construction of the camp would eventually total about $100,000.) All the while, the congregation's officers and trustees worked to finalize plans for the financing and construction of a new Temple. When they were ready at last to present the matter to the membership for a vote, they called a special meeting of the congregation for the evening of Sunday, September 18, 1966. Voting would be by secret ballot, the Board decided, and only those members who attended the meeting would be allowed to participate. No absentee or proxy voting would be permitted.

A mixture of tension and anticipation filled the air on the night of September 18 as some thirteen hundred members, young and old, crowded into the sanctuary at Poplar and Montgomery for the pivotal vote. President Binswanger gaveled the meeting to order at 7:37 p.m., after which Rabbi Danziger offered a special prayer. Next on the agenda was S. L. Kopald, Jr., who

introduced a film that outlined the need for a new Temple. Following the film, Kopald detailed the cost of the project, then estimated to be more than $2.8 million, and announced that the Board and others had already pledged $475,000 toward that goal. Binswanger, a man with an engaging smile and an extraordinarily pleasant demeanor, took the floor again to assure the members that, rumors to the contrary notwithstanding, approval of the resolution to build a new Temple would not involve either an automatic financial assessment or an automatic dues increase. Then Kopald moved the adoption of the resolution to build the new facility.

Kopald's motion opened the floodgates to nearly three hours of discussion and debate. Those in favor of the motion, including Rabbi Wax, spoke of the inadequacies of the existing facility and the inconvenience of its location; those who were against it voiced their concern about the cost of the proposed new Temple, questioned the suitability of the White Station property, and expressed a wistful longing to hold on to the

The sanctuary of the proposed Temple on White Station, as envisioned by architects Gassner, Nathan, and Browne.

grand old building at Poplar and Montgomery, the place where so many congregants had attended religious school, been confirmed, and exchanged their marriage vows. "The very fact that the meeting was held at a site which we all loved so dearly made it very difficult," Herschel Feibelman, then secretary of the congregation, observed later.

As the hour grew late, the members' patience wore thin; courtesy and good will, generally a hallmark of congregational meetings, gave way to frustration and bitterness. It was nearly eleven o'clock when the ballots were finally cast. An IBM machine tabulated the result: 525 votes in favor of the motion, and 740 votes against. The motion failed.

When it was all over, efforts were made to patch up the wounds as quickly as possible. President Binswanger urged the members not to let the issue of a new Temple come between them, but to remain unified in purpose. And Alfred Scharff rose to thank Binswanger for "his ability, fairness, and impartiality, and particularly for the courtesy he showed to each and every person who sought to express himself." Before calling it a night, the members gave Binswanger a standing ovation.

In the weeks that followed, the leaders of Temple Israel were drained. At the next meeting of the Board, when Rudi Scheidt, Sr., proposed that the trustees set aside time at the following month's meeting to "discuss the future of the congregation," he failed to generate even a hint of enthusiasm for the idea. The answer he got from his fellow Board members was short and to the point: "It's too soon."

Still, Scheidt continued to push the Board to try to map out a plan for the congregation's future. In February 1967, after Binswanger retired from the presidency and Julian Allenberg, chairman of Allenberg Parking Stations, Inc., was elected to succeed him, Scheidt got his wish. Under Allenberg's leadership, Board members devoted an entire meeting to mulling over the congregation's dilemma. In the end, though, the solutions they proposed were nothing more than variations on the same old theme: "Temple should build a religious school building out East"; "Temple should build a religious

JULIAN ALLENBERG
Congregation President, 1966-1969

school, youth center, and chapel out East"; "Temple should have facilities both out East and at Poplar and Montgomery"; "Temple should move out East." Nevertheless, Allenberg agreed that the congregation should develop a comprehensive, long-term plan that would encompass its program needs as well as its brick-and-mortar requirements; he appointed Scheidt and Hugh Jacobson to spearhead the effort.

Meanwhile, the Ritual Committee got together for what its chairman, Herbert Glazer, later termed an "old-fashioned bull session." To the surprise of some members of the Board, the views expressed at that meeting revealed an undercurrent of discontent with the style and substance of Temple's religious services. Several committee members candidly admitted they found the services "cold"; others noted that many of the younger members wanted more of the traditional Jewish ritual in the service. One person went so far as to say that Temple Israel, in its resistance to change, was "becoming orthodox in its Reform." The committee recommended a number of changes designed to provide more opportunities for members to participate in services: two or three creative services a year; a candle-lighting ceremony on Friday nights, to be led by members of the Sisterhood; and more music during services, a goal to be achieved, in part, by encouraging the congregation to sing the liturgical responses. One committee member even suggested the congregation should hire a cantor.

All of this was a reflection of the sea change that was taking place at the time in the national Reform Movement. After a century of homogenizing and American-izing its approach to Judaism, the Reform

Movement had begun to recognize the value of certain customs and traditions that were uniquely Jewish. The tide moved slowly at first, but in June 1967, when Israel's decisive, lightning-quick victory in what came to be known as the Six-Day War stirred the pride of Jews all over the world, the pace of change accelerated dramatically. Overnight, it seemed, the image of Jews as perpetual victims faded into the past. One had only to switch on the evening news to see Israel's soldiers — personified by General Moshe Dayan, with his dashing eye-patch — being acclaimed for their heroic exploits. Even in Memphis, people who had never in their lives done anything in public to call attention to their Jewishness found themselves, to their amazement, being congratulated on Israel's victory by their Christian neighbors and business associates.

The events of June 1967 bred a new sense of confidence in America's Jews, along with an intense feeling — new to many in the Reform community — of identity with Israel. So pervasive was this feeling at Temple Israel that two months after the war, the Board urged the Investment Committee to purchase Israel Bonds "to the maximum feasible extent."

By the time the Long-Range Planning Committee issued its report in 1969, Reform Judaism had entered a whole new era. Recommending "greater and more diversified opportunities for involvement for all members," the report endorsed the earlier suggestions of the Ritual Committee and advocated the formation of three new committees: two to deal with traditional areas of interest to Reform Jews — social action and interfaith activities — and one to focus, significantly, on Israel. The report also made a number of recommendations for the religious school that would have been considered heresy just a decade earlier: a required course in Hebrew as part of the curriculum; more emphasis on teaching Torah and Talmud; and the formation, in cooperation with the local Conservative and Orthodox synagogues, of a Jewish Community Educational Institute.

As for the physical plant, the report said the congregation needed a proper auditorium, a separate complex for the high school, a youth lounge, meeting rooms for youth and adults, better office facilities, a teachers' lounge, an adequate bride's room and other wedding facilities, an adequate religious school office, and much more.

"We must provide our members with the opportunity to participate in a forward movement," the long-range report concluded. "Our members yearn for it."

The next man to take the helm of the congregation was Sam Cooper.

Elected to succeed Julian Allenberg in June 1969, Cooper came from a background that was quite different from that of his predecessors: he was a first-generation American who had grown up in the Pinch in an Orthodox family. Though he and his wife, Frankie, had joined Temple in 1947, he was also a lifelong member of two Orthodox congregations, Baron Hirsch and Anshei Sphard. "On the holidays we used to go to three synagogues," Frankie Cooper recalled.

Cooper was a Horatio Alger character come to life. At eighteen, he got a job as an office boy at the company that became HumKo Products — he used to say his first assignment was to sweep the office floor — and through hard work and super salesmanship, he rose to the presidency of HumKo by the time he was forty-one. Along the way he built a reputation as a man who knew how to get things done. "Sam looked at everything in his life as a selling job," Frankie Cooper said of her late husband. "He would never say, 'I can't do it.' It was always, 'It *can* be done.'" Those who worked alongside him on Temple projects soon became

SAM COOPER
Congregation President, 1969-1973
Honorary President, 1993-1999

familiar with his strong-willed personality. "If Sam wanted to do something," one Board member recalled, "*nothing* would stand in his way."

What Cooper wanted to do most during his presidency was to build a new Temple in East Memphis. But first, personnel changes and other matters required his attention. After five years at Temple Israel, Harry Danziger left in the summer of 1969 to become the spiritual leader of Temple B'nai Israel in Monroe, Louisiana. Shortly afterward a new assistant rabbi, Howard Schwartz, joined the staff. Harvey Kaye, a new educational director for the religious school, also started working at Temple in the summer of 1969. He would stay until 1977.

In 1970 the Southwest Region of the Union of American Hebrew Congregations (UAHC) celebrated the opening of the Henry S. Jacobs Camp in Utica, Mississippi. Named for the executive director of Temple Sinai in New Orleans, the camp was a dream come true for many Jewish leaders in the region. Among them: Rabbi Solomon Kahn Kaplan, the founding director of the Southwest Region of the UAHC (and the father of John Kaplan, who would later become Temple Israel's cantor); Ben Sklar of Ruleville, Mississippi, and Celeste Orkin of Jackson, Mississippi, who, along with others in the small Jewish communities in the Mid-South, worked long and hard to drum up support for the camp and keep the venture alive; and former Temple Israel president Julian Allenberg, who was instrumental in raising $400,000 to get the camp completed. Under the leadership of Macy B. Hart, its first director, the Jacobs camp fulfilled its promise from the start, creating a wealth of meaningful Reform Jewish experiences for children, teens, and adults throughout the Mid-South.

Meanwhile, Rabbi Wax and the leaders of Temple Israel also were exploring new ways to experience Reform Judaism. By 1970 they had introduced a number of new programs — a Hebrew class for all fourth-graders in the religious school, for example, and special worship services to commemorate the Holocaust and celebrate Israel Independence Day. Still, Wax wanted to proceed cautiously. Embracing change without abandoning the cherished precepts of Classical Reform, he realized, was going to be quite a balancing act. "We are engaged in experimentation, as are other congregations, but [we] find it difficult to know precisely what changes we should make," the rabbi acknowledged at the annual meeting in 1970. He added, however, "We are cognizant of the fact that we need a new approach to keep our youth interested in Judaism."

One new approach Wax initially opposed was the hiring of a cantor. Nevertheless, in 1970, at the urging of the Choir Committee, chaired by H. Kirke Lewis, he agreed to invite three Reform cantors to visit Temple. Each cantor participated in Friday night services and then stayed over to work with the children in the religious school on Sunday. "Not one of the children in my class failed to respond enthusiastically to the musical leadership of the three cantors who visited us," one teacher wrote to President Sam Cooper at the end of that year. The teacher continued: "Several of the children asked why we could not have a cantor at Temple Israel. Some even suggested the cantor could teach their parents the songs they learned in their classrooms if he were present in the Friday night services. And I, during the sessions with the cantors, felt closer to Judaism than I have since my last SoFTY friendship circle." [84]

Faced with such a positive response, Wax eventually came to agree there could be a role — albeit a very limited one — for a cantor at Temple Israel. "Cantors are a part of Reform Judaism, and some of the most distinctive Reform temples have cantors," he assured the members of the Board, some of whom were clearly uncomfortable with what they called "this fundamental change." A cantor will "enrich the service," Wax added, and "will benefit our children."

So it was that in 1971, the ever-cheerful Thomas Schwartz joined the Temple staff as its first full-time cantor/music director in approximately eighty years. His salary for the first year did not come out of the Temple budget; rather, it was funded privately by a group of members who were so convinced a cantor would have a positive impact on the congregation, and especially on the children, they were willing to pay him out of their own pockets.

Meanwhile, behind the scenes, Sam Cooper kept trying to make some kind of headway toward his primary goal of relocating the Temple to East Memphis. But in spite of his efforts, that goal remained frustratingly out of reach. In 1970, following on the heels of a successful $2 million campaign by the Memphis Jewish Community Center to construct a new building in the 6000 block of Poplar Avenue, the leaders of the congregation tried again to raise the necessary $3 million to build a new Temple out East. But they failed, again.

With great reluctance, the Temple's officers and trustees concluded they would have to settle for the proverbial "half a loaf": they endorsed a proposal to build a youth facility, religious school, chapel, and auditorium on the White Station property, and for the moment, at least, to keep the sanctuary at Poplar and Montgomery. At a special meeting on September 20, 1970 — a meeting that drew less than one-third of the members who had attended that contentious gathering four years earlier — the congregation approved the plan. It turned out, however, that many members were unwilling to lend their financial support to an arrangement that would leave them with a religious school out East and a sanctuary in Midtown. So once again the leaders were stymied.

It was at this juncture, just when the situation was beginning to seem hopeless, that Sam Cooper won the support of Abe Plough. On September 7, 1971, Plough invited a group of the congregation's leaders and major contributors to a dinner at the Summit Club, at which he issued a challenge: if the fifteen top donors to the Building Fund would raise their gifts to a total of $1 million (more than twice as much as they had already pledged), and if the remaining members of the congregation would contribute a total of $1.5 million (of which about

ABE PLOUGH
Honorary President, 1972-1984

$1 million in cash and pledges, including a $100,000 pledge from the Sisterhood, had already been received), then the Plough Family Foundation would contribute $1 million to the Building Fund. This would enable the congregation to raise $3.5 million, the amount needed to go forward with the design and construction of a complete new facility in East Memphis.

It was exactly the jump-start the stalled campaign needed. Within a month the fifteen largest donors met Plough's challenge, and on the strength of their commitment, the Board once again approved a proposal to build a new Temple in East Memphis. On November 14, 1971, the congregation held yet another special meeting — the third such gathering in five years — but this time the proceedings were short and sweet. Sam Cooper called the members to order at 7:30 p.m., and by 8:45 they were on their way back home again, having voted overwhelmingly in favor of building a new Temple.

It was Abe Plough's challenge gift, of course, that had made all the difference. Six months later, as a gesture of gratitude, the congregation named him honorary president for life. (The position had been vacant since Joseph Lewis's death in 1965.) As to what had inspired Plough to change his mind about the need for a new Temple, a project for which he had displayed little or no enthusiasm during the previous decade, former President S.L. Kopald, Jr., later offered a simple explanation: "The timing was finally right," he said. Then, with a self-deprecating chuckle, he added, "And Sam Cooper was a better salesman than I was."

Once the congregation had approved the proposal to build a new Temple, the appropriate committees swung into action. By now there was general agreement that the White Station property was unsuitable, so the Site Selection Committee went hunting for a better location. Among the properties they considered: a fifteen-acre tract on Yates Road that was part of the John S. King estate; a seventy-acre property, then owned by Norfleet R. Turner, at the corner of Shady Grove and Sweetbrier; and a twenty-six acre tract at Walnut Grove and I-240, owned by Baptist Hospital. At one point Abe Plough quietly — and unsuccessfully — submitted a bid for a choice piece of land on the east side of Sweetbrier, just north of Poplar; the winning bidder, whose offer was just a fraction higher than Plough's, purchased the land for Briarcrest Baptist School.

Then, tucked away in the center of a residential neighborhood, amid thirty acres of lush greenery, towering oaks, and gently rolling hills, Temple Israel found its new home. Originally part of a sixty-acre tract, the property on East Massey Road had once belonged to Raymond Firestone, a member of the family that founded Firestone Tire and Rubber Co., which had opened a factory in Memphis in the late 1930s. By the time Temple Israel became interested in the property, the perimeter of the tract had been sold off to the developers of the Eastwood Manor subdivision. The house and grounds in the center were held in trust for the heirs of Robert Galloway, who had bought the property from Firestone.

This time the Board took no chances: its bid of $700,000, or more than $23,000 an acre, easily topped the $450,000 offer submitted by Universal Financial and Investment Corporation, the only other bidder for the property. The sale closed on November 15, 1973.

Meanwhile, the congregation's property on White Station Road turned out to have been a wise investment, if not an ideal location for a new Temple. In August 1973, former President William Loewenberg presented the Board with a contract from Kindle (Bud) Davis, owner of the Bud Davis Cadillac dealership, for $1 million in cash. When the sale closed in early September, the money was invested in a 120-day certificate of deposit bearing a whopping 10.87 percent interest per year. The congregation would continue to reap the benefits of rising interest rates throughout the inflationary 1970s, earning additional income to be used for the new Temple. At the same time, however, construction costs also continued to spiral upward.

In August 1973 Sam Cooper retired from the presidency, but not from the action. He merely switched hats, taking over the crucial chairmanship of the New Temple Building Fund. Thus it would fall to real estate attorney Herschel Feibelman, just as it had to Joseph Strauss, Elias Lowenstein, and Joseph Newburger before him, to shepherd the congregation through the construction process and lead it into a new house of worship.

HERSCHEL FEIBELMAN
Congregation President, 1973-1977

Feibelman, a longtime chairman of the Religious School Committee, had been among the first to recognize the need for the Temple to move to East Memphis, where the majority of the congregation now lived. As president, he would devote his heart and soul over the next four years to making that dream become a reality.

One of the first tasks on Feibelman's agenda was to find a buyer for the old Temple at Poplar and Montgomery. The Board set a price of $1 million on the property, and for more than a year, no offers came their way. Then, in October 1974, a man named Gray Allison entered the picture. "Mr. Allison, who was then a resident of Little Rock, had $30,000, two brothers who were doctors of philosophy in religion, and sixteen students," Feibelman recalled, "and they wanted to establish what was to be called the Mid-South Baptist Theological Seminary." Though Allison's prospects did not sound very promising, Feibelman agreed to listen to his proposal. In due course a meeting was arranged: Feibelman and former President William Loewenberg negotiated for Temple, and Allison, along with Roland Maddox and Rev. Adrian Rogers from Bellevue Baptist Church (then located in Midtown), represented the would-be theological seminary. Over breakfast at the old Admiral Benbow Inn on Union Avenue, the five men sat down to try to work out a deal. Loewenberg offered

After finalizing the sale of the "old Temple," the principals posed for the camera. (**LEFT TO RIGHT**) *Roland Maddox, Gene Howard, and Morris Mills, representing Mid-America Baptist Theological Seminary; Abe Plough, Sam Cooper, William Loewenberg, Herschel Feibelman, and Rabbi James Wax representing Temple Israel; Dr. Gray Allison, president of the seminary.*

to knock off the equivalent of the real estate commission, bringing the $1 million asking price down to $940,000. Rogers said his group could raise $800,000 (including the $30,000 Allison had in hand), but no more. That left a gap of $140,000 between the seller and the buyer.

Later that day, at Loewenberg's suggestion, Feibelman went to see Abe Plough, the only person the two men could think of who could bridge that gap. As he had done so many times in the past, Plough responded to the need; he agreed to make a donation of $140,000 to enable the seminary to meet Temple's asking price.

Under the terms of the contract, the congregation would retain possession of the building while its new facility was under construction. The contract also specified certain items the congregation wanted to take with it from the old Temple, including the Torahs, the cornerstone, the eternal light, the Ten Commandments etched in marble, the memorial boards, and all the books in the library. Later on, the Board also asked to take the ornamental ark doors from the sanctuary.

The sale of the old Temple, together with the sale of the property on White Station Road, added some $2 million to the Building Fund, paving the way for the congregation finally to embark on the construction of its new facility. Gassner, Nathan, and Browne, the architectural firm that had worked on plans for the White Station site a decade earlier, was hired once again to design the new Temple, this time in consultation with Percival Goodman of New York, one of the nation's most prolific synagogue architects. (Temple Israel was one of the last buildings designed by Francis Gassner, the lead architect on the project, who died in 1977 at the age of fifty.

The 1975 groundbreaking ceremony for the new Temple on East Massey.
TOP (LEFT TO RIGHT): Sisterhood President LaVerne Siegel, Brotherhood President Arthur Lettes, Junior Congregation President Nancy Schneider.
MIDDLE: Amy Allenberg, Pearl Felsenthal, and Louise Lewis, whose husbands had served as president of the congregation. BOTTOM: President Herschel Feibelman and Associate Rabbi Harry Danziger.

Temple Israel's trustees and staff at the groundbreaking ceremony: FRONT ROW (LEFT TO RIGHT): *LaVerne Siegel, Rabbi Harry Danziger, Leo Bearman, Sr., Sam Cooper, Rabbi James Wax, Abe Plough, Herschel Feibelman, William Loewenberg, Mildred Schwartz.* MIDDLE ROW: *Irvin Bogatin, Richard Orgel, Arlene Schwartz, Bert Barnett, Eugene Goldberg, Jerrold Graber, Robert Goldsmith, Leo Bearman, Jr., Herbert Kohn, Lenore Binswanger, Milton Binswanger, Jr., Joan White, Larry Lewis, Sanford Lichterman, Lawrence Halperin, H. Kirke Lewis, Arthur Lettes, Sam Haspel, Jr., Tim Malkin, Executive Director Joe Boston, Nick Ringel, Educational Director Harvey Kaye.* BACK ROW: *S.L. Kopald, Jr., Dr. Marvin Gottlieb, James Jalenak, Nancy Schneider, Hermine Davidson, Irving Strauch, Mel Olswanger, Herbert Benham, Eugene Greener, Max Notowitz, Rudi Scheidt, Sr., Maurice Buchalter, Leslie Gruber.*

Gassner's memorial service was held in the sanctuary of the new Temple; though he was not Jewish, he had come to regard Temple Israel as his spiritual home.)

At the suggestion of Abe Plough, the Board engaged a construction consultant for the new Temple named Carl A. Morse, a tough New Yorker who had been involved in the construction of Plough, Inc.'s headquarters and several other large office buildings in Memphis, and whose company, Morse/Diesel, Inc., had taken part in the construction of the Pan Am Building in New York and the Sears Tower in Chicago. Then, in January 1975, the Board approved the selection of the Frank J. Rooney Co. of Miami, Florida, as general contractor. Alfred Alperin, chairman of the Building Committee, reported that the "fast track" method of construction would be used — that is, subcontractors

would be hired without the time-consuming process of competitive bidding.

Over the next eighteen months, scores of Temple members served on committees related to the building of the new Temple, and just about everyone wound up with a favorite story to tell about the experience. For Feibelman, who visited the construction site nearly every day, as did his wife, Shirley, those anecdotes focused on two unforgettable men. The first of these was Haskell "Charlie" Lieberman, the Rooney Company's construction foreman, who was "as rough and tough as anybody needed to be," Feibelman recalled. The first time they met, Lieberman was supervising a small crew of men who were clearing the construction site with a bulldozer. "As I came up," Feibelman said, "Lieberman had snatched the driver of the bulldozer off of his vehicle, and he said, 'You son of a b_____! I told you if you hit a tree, I was going to hit *you!*' And he did!" After that, Feibelman noted with a chuckle, the crews were careful not to cause any unnecessary damage to the trees on the Temple property. Lieberman's insistence on quality workmanship extended to the interior of the building as well. "I think we had some 160 carpenters who worked on the building at various times," Feibelman said. "Sixty of them worked only a half-day. He [Lieberman] looked at their work and it didn't satisfy him, so out they went." When the construction was complete, the Temple Board made Charlie Lieberman an honorary member of the congregation.[95]

Feibelman also had vivid memories of Carl Morse, the construction consultant, another man who insisted on nothing but the best in workmanship and materials. Even when his demands drove up the cost of construction — as did his insistence, given the city's proximity to the New Madrid Fault, on incorporating earthquake-resistant features that went far beyond the building code requirements at the time — Morse stuck to his guns. "Don't you worry about it," he told Feibelman when the congregation's president questioned the extra expense of the Temple's seismic foundation. "If it gets us into trouble, Abe [Plough] and I will work it out."[96] (More than a quarter-century after it was built, Temple Israel was still considered one of the most earthquake-resistant public buildings in Shelby County.) Morse worked on the Temple project for a nominal fee, largely as a favor to Plough, and when the job was finished, he and his wife, Belle, made a $25,000 contribution to the Temple Israel Building Fund.

Plough himself was not involved in the construction on a day-to-day basis and rarely attended Board or committee meetings. He did, however, turn up at one particular Sunday morning meeting of the Building Fund Committee, much to the surprise of the others who were there. The meeting originally had been scheduled to take place at the construction site, but when a heavy downpour turned the East Massey property into a sea of mud, Joe Boston, the Temple's executive director, called the committee members and instructed them to meet at Sam Cooper's office in the White Station Tower instead. Boston neglected, however, to call Abe Plough, reasoning that since Plough almost always skipped these meetings, there was no need to notify him of the last-minute location change.

To everyone's embarrassment, the Temple's most generous benefactor turned up at Cooper's office about forty minutes after the meeting had begun, impeccably dressed in a business suit, but with his shoes, socks, and trousers caked with mud. "Nobody called *me* to let me know the meeting was changed," Plough barked, standing in the doorway. The committee members were speechless. "We all held our breath, waiting to see what would happen next," recalled Nick Ringel, a member of the fund-raising committee. "But Sam Cooper never missed a beat. He just greeted Mr. Plough with a big smile and said, 'Abe! We're so glad you could join us! Come on over here and have a seat next to me.' So Mr. Plough sat down, and the meeting continued as though nothing had happened."

Determined to have the congregation enter its new Temple free of debt, Plough kept a close eye on the Building Fund during the entire time the Temple was under construction. In January 1976, when it became apparent that an additional $1 million would be needed to complete the new facility, he issued a new challenge, promising to match every dollar paid into the Building Fund up to a total of $500,000. And a few months after the Temple was completed, he quietly covered an additional $286,000 in construction expenses. In the end, the cost of building and furnishing the Temple on East

Massey totaled nearly $7 million, of which Abe Plough and the Plough Foundation contributed nearly 30 percent.

And so it came to pass, after twenty years of planning and prodding, that the Temple Israel family bade farewell to the Midtown building that had been its spiritual home for sixty years and moved to East Memphis. On September 10, 1976, Rabbi Wax led the congregation through its last Friday night worship service at the old Temple, an occasion of teary nostalgia and high drama that culminated with the stirring sounds of the shofar.

The following weekend was devoted to a three-day dedication of the new Temple, a sleek, contemporary building nestled in the center of thirty acres of park-like surroundings. Designed with warmth and beauty and elegant simplicity, the new house of worship featured a wide atrium at the entrance, a welcoming space that provided a peaceful transition from the secular to the sacred. The sanctuary, created in the shape of a half-circle, offered an abundance of seating close to the *bimah*. The half-circle also served as a metaphor for the congregation's relationship to the community, implying that the members have a

responsibility to carry out God's commandments not only within the sanctuary walls, but also in the world beyond those walls — the other half of the circle, as it were — in order to be complete.

To the left of the main entrance stood an intimate chapel, where the ark doors, the eternal light, and the Ten Commandments brought from the old Temple found a new home in front of a wall-to-wall, floor-to-

ceiling tapestry woven in brilliant colors. The spacious new facility also had a large social hall, thirty-two well-lighted classrooms, and an abundance of office space for the rabbinical, religious school, and administrative staff. New York artist Efrem Weitzman had been commissioned to design many of the Temple's distinctive visual features, including the interior of the sanctuary ark and its bronze doors, which evoked the

Burning Bush; the mosaic walls flanking the ark; the stained glass windows and skylights in the sanctuary, foyer, and chapel; and the vivid tapestry and ark in the chapel. (Later, Weitzman designed two more pieces for Temple Israel as a gift from the Sisterhood: a menorah for the mosaic wall in the sanctuary and a stylized *Shema* for the Temple's exterior wall.)

Five separate events were held to dedicate the new synagogue, including a special service for the Junior Congregation and religious school, an open house for residents of the surrounding neighborhood, a program for members of the other synagogues in Memphis, and another one for the community at large. But by far the most memorable occasion took place on Friday, September 17, 1976, when the congregation gathered for the first Sabbath eve service in the new Temple. Brimming with pride and fulfillment, the officers and trustees of the congregation led a procession of past presidents, rabbis, the cantor, and distinguished guests down the aisle of the new sanctuary, carrying the Torahs to their new home. Two leaders of the American Reform Movement — Rabbi Alexander M. Schindler, president of the Union of American Hebrew Congregations, and Rabbi Alfred

The Ten Commandments, eternal light, and ark doors from the old Temple found a new home in the chapel on East Massey.

Gottschalk, president of Hebrew Union College-Jewish Institute of Religion — were on hand for the occasion, along with Rabbi Jacob Rader Marcus, dean of American Jewish historians and director of the American Jewish Archives, and Bonia Shur, director of Liturgic Arts at Hebrew Union College-Jewish

Institute of Religion, who had composed and arranged special music for the dedication.

If ever there was a moment that called for a *Shehecheyanu*, this was it. More than a few members of the Temple family grew misty-eyed as they stood together, congregation and clergy, and recited the traditional Jewish prayer of thanksgiving, slightly altered for the occasion: "Blessed art Thou, Lord our God, King of the Universe, who has kept us in life, sustained us, and brought us to this sacred and happy hour in the history of our beloved Temple Israel."

Back in the spring of 1973, three and one-half years before that historic Friday night when the new Temple was dedicated, Rabbi Wax and Sam Cooper had sat down together for a long talk.

The time had come, Wax said, to begin planning for his retirement — which meant the time had also come for Temple Israel to designate his successor. Ordinarily, this would have been Cooper's cue to organize a search committee, but in this instance both he and Wax had another plan in mind: call Harry Danziger.

Danziger, in fact, was number one on just about everybody's list of possible successors to the venerable James Wax. During the five years he had spent at Temple Israel when he was fresh out of rabbinical school, he had developed an enthusiastic following among old and young alike. His sermons, delivered in an informal, conversational tone, were both witty and wise. He had a gift for saying the right thing in almost any situation. And he was adept at bringing diverse groups of people together and making everyone feel comfortable. The latter was a skill he may have picked up from his father, Rabbi Jacob Danziger, who had for many years successfully bridged the gap between the Orthodox and Conservative factions of his own congregation in Huntington, West Virginia.

HARRY K. DANZIGER
Spiritual Leader of Temple Israel, 1978-2000

By 1973 Danziger and his family had moved to Baltimore, where he was serving as the associate rabbi of Temple Oheb Shalom. He accepted the call to return to Memphis, and on April 23, 1973, the Temple's Board of Trustees made it official: they elected Harry Danziger to the position of associate rabbi (to succeed Rabbi Richard Birnholz, who had notified the Board he would be leaving in June of that year), and they recommended "that there be a continuity of service by Rabbi Danziger, ultimately resulting in his being . . . elected senior rabbi of the congregation upon the retirement of Dr. Wax in the spring of 1978."

Arriving back in Memphis in the summer of 1973, Danziger used his Rosh Hashanah sermon in September of that year to state his principles and spell out his mission, just as Wax himself had done on a Rosh Hashanah morning nearly three decades earlier. But whereas Wax on that occasion had earnestly endorsed "a religion that emphasizes righteousness and not ritual," Danziger now just as earnestly called for a renewed emphasis on ritual, personal observance, and symbols in Jewish life. It was time, he said, for the members of Temple Israel to revive some of the Jewish traditions their forebears had discarded over the years in their eagerness to be accepted in America — traditions like studying Torah, going to the synagogue to say *Kaddish* for a departed loved one, fasting on Yom Kippur, having a *bris* for a baby boy.

"I'm not calling for a return to Orthodoxy," Danziger assured the members of Temple Israel. "I *am* saying that we can afford to look Jewish after all these years and that, out of self-respect alone, we cannot afford not to."[97]

In that 1973 "Trunk in the Attic" sermon — so-called because of the image Danziger conjured up of Jewish immigrants shedding their religious customs when they arrived in America and packing them away in "a trunk in the attic" — the designated successor to Rabbi Wax let it be known that Classical Reform would gradually become a thing of the past at Temple Israel. While he did not spell out exactly what changes he would make, or when and how he would make them, the message was clear: with Harry Danziger as their spiritual guide, the members of Temple Israel were going to haul that trunk out of the attic and start rediscovering their Jewish roots.

Before any of that could take place, however, turmoil erupted once again in the Middle East. On the morning of Yom Kippur, which fell on Saturday, October 6, that year, Egypt and Syria launched a surprise attack against Israel, catching the beleaguered nation so unprepared that in the early stages of the conflict the outcome was very much in doubt. With Israel's existence at stake, Jewish communities around the world shifted into overdrive to respond to the crisis. In Memphis, hasty arrangements were made for a pro-Israel rally to be held at Baron Hirsch on Monday, October 8. Among the organizing groups was the Temple Israel Brotherhood, whose members telephoned the entire congregation in the space of two days to urge everyone to attend. At the meeting itself, speaker after speaker took the podium to hammer home the urgency of the situation, but it was none other than Rabbi Wax — a man not previously known to champion Israel's cause — who brought the overflow crowd to its feet with an impassioned speech in support of the Jewish homeland. The Temple Board also came to Israel's aid, using $250,000 from the Building Fund to purchase State of Israel Bonds.

When the crisis passed, the congregation focused once again on matters close to home. The next few years were busy ones: Rabbi Wax readied himself for retirement, Rabbi Danziger prepared to steer the congregation in new directions, and the lay leadership completed the gigantic task of raising the money for the new Temple and supervising its construction.

Even before the facility on East Massey was built, one could sense a rising tide of interest and enthusiasm among the membership. In 1973-74, Ray Ann Kremer chaired a series of Jewish Experiential Workshops that brought together a cross-section of members. The participants shared their thoughts about what they could do for Temple and, of equal importance, what they expected Temple to do for them. To Danziger, the workshops were "the most exciting thing going on in the congregation" when he arrived back at Temple Israel in 1973. "The idea that people were being asked . . . what is the Jew in you, and what does the Jew in you want and need," he recalled, "*that* was a watershed." In response to those questions, nearly all the workshop participants expressed a desire for more opportunities for involvement by the members. Many also said they wished the congregation offered a greater sense of community.

Three years later, Danziger incorporated those wishes into a comprehensive proposal for programs to begin in 1976-77, the congregation's first year in its new home. Meeting with the Board on a Sunday morning in May 1976, he offered a broad line-up of new activities designed to meet the needs of every age group in the congregation: alternative worship services, especially for young people; "shared Jewish experiences," such as congregational Chanukah celebrations and one-day retreats for bar/bat mitzvah families; midweek daytime and evening study sessions; business people's lunches; retirees' breakfasts; cultural events; a committee on "intra-Jewish activities"; new social action programs. "We had so much possibility," Danziger said years later, recalling the eagerness of the congregation as it prepared to make the move to East Massey. "The pressure was all there, and all [that was] required was to provide opportunities."

And provide them he did. In November 1976 Danziger and his wife, Jeanne, led twenty-four Temple members on a two-week tour of Israel, the first trip to Israel ever sponsored by the congregation. The following year the Israeli Chasidic Song Festival came to Memphis to perform at Temple Israel; the event, jointly

More than two dozen congregants joined the Danzigers for the second Temple Israel-sponsored trip to Israel in 1978.

sponsored by the Jewish Federation, the Jewish Community Center, and all four local synagogues, drew a sell-out crowd. In 1977 the congregation conducted its first annual bar/bat mitzvah workshop, an occasion that culminated with a ceremony in the chapel at which each participant was given the Torah portion he or she would recite on the big day. In addition, each bar/bat mitzvah candidate was "twinned" with a child of a Jewish "refusenik" in the Soviet Union. The Memphis youngsters were asked to correspond with their counterparts in the Soviet Union, where the practice of Judaism was forbidden at that time, and symbolically share their bar/bat mitzvahs with them.

In a different vein, Temple's Community Affairs Committee in 1977 presented a series of programs titled "Conflicts," in which hot topics in the news, such as the Bakke anti-affirmative action case then under consideration by the U.S. Supreme Court, were discussed. And the Temple Sisterhood launched its first Mother's Day Out program, offering child-care two days a week. Intended as a boon for busy parents, the program, later known as Noah's Ark, provided the added benefit of familiarizing the children of Temple members with Jewish traditions — holidays, prayers, songs, symbols — at a very early age.

For the first time in years, the congregation's membership increased when it moved to East Memphis, growing from its previous level of about 1,350 families, where it had remained static since the mid-1960s, to more than 1,450 families in 1977. According to a census conducted by the local Jewish Federation, more than half the ten thousand Jews in Memphis were now affiliated with Temple Israel.

Thus it was with a sense of "mission accomplished" that James A. Wax assumed the status of rabbi emeritus in March 1978, leaving an indelible imprint not only on the congregation he had served for thirty-two years, but also on the city as a whole. He would go on to lead an active retirement — writing, lecturing, and traveling several times a year to Helena, Arkansas, to lead services at that city's small Reform congregation, Temple Beth El. Wax was in the middle of his Yom Kippur sermon there on October 8, 1989 — preaching, characteristically, that it is immoral to deprive poor people of access to adequate health-care — when he collapsed from a ruptured aneurysm. He died in Memphis nine days later.

Of the many civic and religious leaders who praised Wax's life and hailed his legacy, it was his friend and colleague, the Rev. Frank McRae, pastor of St. John's United Methodist Church, who offered what was perhaps the best summation of Wax's lasting impact on the community. "Jews are better Jews and Christians are better Christians," McRae said simply, "because Jimmy was around."[98]

Using funds that were contributed in Wax's memory, the Board of Temple Israel established two new programs designed to perpetuate the spirit of his rabbinate: the James A. Wax Institute for the Clergy, which would bring members of the local clergy to Temple every other year for a morning of lectures and fellowship, and the James A. Wax Social Justice Sabbath, through which the congregation would have an opportunity to hear speakers nationally known for their work in behalf of human rights and dignity. In November 1990, in conjunction with the first Social Justice Sabbath, the congregation dedicated the social hall at Temple in memory of Wax and his predecessor, Harry W. Ettelson, officially designating it the Ettelson-Wax Hall.

By the time Harry Danziger was installed as senior rabbi of Temple Israel on April 7, 1978, ten years had passed since the assassination of Martin Luther King, Jr.

The decade had brought momentous events to Temple Israel, but for Memphis as a whole it had been a difficult and dismal ten years.

Downtown Memphis, once the heart of the city's retail district, had taken on the appearance of a ghost town in the wake of the King assassination. Faced with deteriorating business conditions, most downtown store owners had either moved to more promising locations or called it quits entirely, leaving boarded-up windows and empty buildings to scar the landscape. Even the city's landmark hotel, The Peabody, had eventually closed its doors. Still smarting from having been described by *Time* magazine in 1968 as "a decaying Mississippi River town," Memphis dropped below the nation's radar during the 1970s.[99] Had Elvis Presley not died at Graceland in 1977, the rest of the country would have taken no notice of Memphis at all.

Civic boosters tried valiantly to encourage optimism, insisting that just as the city had managed to reverse its downward spiral in the aftermath of the yellow fever epidemics, it could also rebound from these current setbacks. But the future was uncertain, at best. Even those with the rosiest of rose-colored glasses did not dare to dream that over the next two decades, their downtrodden city could — and would — blossom into a thriving, multi-cultural metropolis with a population of over a million.

One of the early mileposts on the road to recovery came in 1972, when Memphian Frederick W. Smith launched a nationwide overnight delivery service called Federal Express, disregarding the professor at Yale University who had told him, so the story goes, that his

Photo by Jack E. Boucher, courtesy Library of Congress

Boarded-up windows and empty buildings: Beale Street, looking west from South Third Street, 1974.

pioneering business concept would never work. The success of FedEx put Memphis on the map as a strategically located distribution center, helped coax other national companies to set up operations in Memphis, and prompted, in due course, an expansion of the city's airport. By the mid-1980s, the Memphis airport would be one of Northwest Airlines' three domestic hubs, and by the end of the '90s it would rank number one in the world in the handling of air cargo.

Downtown itself began to come back to life when real estate entrepreneur Jack Belz and his father, Philip, having acquired The Peabody in a foreclosure sale, decided to take a gamble and develop the property. After remodeling and refurbishing the grand old hotel from top to bottom, they reopened it in 1981 — complete with its famous ducks — to widespread acclaim. A year later a theme park and museum opened on Mud Island, an overgrown sandbar in the Mississippi River that had sat for decades, ugly and largely unused, at the city's front door. And a year after that, a renovated Beale Street once again began sporting restaurants and blues clubs. Over the next twenty years, the trickle of development that began with The Peabody grew into a torrent of renovation and new construction: at the north end of downtown, the Pyramid arena; at the south end, the National Civil Rights Museum; and in between, such amenities as the Orpheum, a restored theater for touring Broadway shows; AutoZone Park, a new baseball stadium for the Class AAA Memphis Redbirds; the Peabody Place mall and entertainment complex; the Smithsonian Institution's "Rock 'N Soul" museum; and the Cannon Center for the Performing Arts. Meanwhile, a growing number of Memphians even discovered the pleasures of living downtown — on Mud Island in a new residential community called Harbortown, and in condos, loft apartments, and even single-family homes sprinkled

The marble fountain in The Peabody's lobby provides a playground for the hotel's signature ducks.

along city streets and on the river bluffs.

At the same time, many other area residents were choosing to settle in the far reaches of Shelby County, and even beyond, fueling a wave of subdivision and shopping mall construction that created an abundance of job opportunities. Drawn by the area's growing economy, thousands of Hispanics, Asians, and other ethnic groups moved to Memphis during the latter part of the twentieth century, adding spice — literally! — to the area's cultural milieu. By the end of the 1990s, the city's dining scene, not previously noted for its variety, boasted a handful of Indian restaurants, dozens of Mexican/Latin American eateries, and more than fifty establishments specializing in Chinese, Japanese, Thai, Korean, or Vietnamese cuisine.

Perhaps no segment of Memphis benefited more from the city's economic growth than its African-American community. True, many of the city's black citizens remained undereducated and underemployed during the 1980s and '90s, but many others took advantage of the opportunities created by the civil rights movement and transitioned into the middle class. While lingering distrust between the races continued to haunt Memphis's civic agenda throughout the period, the black community did, in fact, make significant progress in most aspects of city life — especially in the political arena. Memphis elected its first black mayor, Dr. Willie W. Herenton, in 1991, and thirteen years later he was still in office, having won the support of both black and white Memphians for an unprecedented fourth term.

It was against this backdrop of enormous growth and change that Harry Danziger served as the spiritual leader of Temple Israel. During his twenty-two year tenure, as Memphis and the rest of the nation became more aware of ethnic, cultural, and religious differences — and more accepting of them — Danziger made important modifications of his own at Temple Israel, inspired by the shift of emphasis that was already underway in the Reform Movement.

His goal, as he had suggested in his 1973 "Trunk in the Attic" sermon, was to bring Temple Israel into line with middle-of-the-road Reform Judaism. "A big part of my thinking," he would say later, "was that the kids who were growing up at Temple Israel in Memphis were not all going to live at Temple Israel in Memphis. They were going to go out into a Jewish world where, for lack of a better word, we were on a wing of it, as opposed to being in the mainstream" — a Jewish world where, he feared, the kids from Temple Israel would "feel they don't belong." So the congregation's seventh senior rabbi set out to expand Temple Israel's Jewish horizons, to open the members' eyes to the broad spectrum of

Downtown Memphis reborn, circa 2001

what the Reform Movement now had to offer.

Not all the changes Danziger would implement over the next two decades involved customs and ritual. The first item on his agenda was simply to make the prevailing atmosphere at Temple Israel less formal. "This was a big, imposing, building," he said, thinking back to the congregation's first few years on East Massey. "If we had brought people into this building and also given them the sense of great formality, and [the perception that] 'you'd better work hard to feel like you belong here,' they'd find another place to go. So it had to be warm and welcoming." Working to dispel the notion that Temple Israel was a place where, in his words, "everybody has known everybody forever," Danziger started showing up at new member dinners and Board retreats with a map of the United States under his arm. He'd set the map on an easel and then go around the room introducing everyone, putting a pin in the map to mark each person's hometown. The exercise worked well as an icebreaker, and it provided a concrete demonstration of the congregation's growing diversity. Around this time Danziger also began referring to the membership not just as a "congregation," but as a "congregational family," a warm, inclusive phrase designed to help both longtime members and newcomers feel at home.

It was Danziger's re-introduction of certain traditional religious practices, however, that brought about the most dramatic transformation at Temple Israel. A strategic thinker, the rabbi planned the ritual changes carefully, and in the beginning, at least, he implemented them gradually. Rarely, if ever, did he discuss a particular change in advance. "The less [the members] were told about [a change]," he would say later, "and the less it was suggested that this was a *big* change, the more easily it was accepted. So I never billed something as a big change."

Among the early changes was a gradual transition from the Ashkenazic (European) pronunciation of Hebrew, which had been in use at Temple Israel ever since the congregation was established, to the Sephardic (Spanish/Middle Eastern) dialect, the official language of modern-day Israel. One Friday night, to demonstrate the differences between the two dialects, Danziger and the congregation's then-assistant rabbi, Alan Greenbaum, engaged in an Ashkenazic-Sephardic dialogue from the pulpit. "I said 'Good *Shabbos*' to him," Danziger recalled, "and he said '*Shabbat Shalom*' to me, and we went on like that throughout the service." Overall, he said, it took several years for the congregation to become accustomed to hearing and reciting the Sephardic dialect.

Even more carefully orchestrated was Danziger's introduction in 1979 of a new prayer book, *Gates of Prayer*, which replaced the old *Union Prayer Book* that had been the mainstay of Reform congregations, including Temple Israel, for as long as anyone could remember. Knowing there was substantial opposition in the congregation to the new prayer book, Danziger took a methodical, step-by-step approach, starting out by giving the members what he called "a positive experience with the literature" — that is, he read some of the most appealing passages from the new book during *Shabbat* (formerly known as "*Shabbos*" or "Sabbath") services, being sure to mention that the excerpts had come from the new *Gates of Prayer*. After a while he began using *Gates of Prayer* every other week, but he left the old *Union Prayer Books* in the seat racks and had the ushers hand out the new books on the occasions when they were needed. Still later he reversed the procedure, leaving the new books in the racks and handing out the old ones on the alternate weeks. Finally, after the bar mitzvah of Edward Felsenthal, the last student at Temple who was trained in the *Union Prayer Book*, Danziger instructed the Temple staff to "put away the old *Union Prayer Books* and let's see if anybody asks about it." No one did.

As time went on, Danziger occasionally tested the congregation's readiness to adopt a particular ritual simply by inviting worshippers on a Friday night to join him in observing it. Such was the case the first time he chanted the Torah blessings, instead of reading them as he had always done in the past. That the congregation was indeed ready for the change became patently clear, he said, when "a chorus of people" chanted the ancient melody right along with him. On other occasions Danziger would simply surprise the congregation by wearing something new — a *tallit* (the Sephardic pronunciation of *tallis*), for example — or doing something new, such as marching the Torahs out into the congregation, without saying anything about it. At such times, he said, the message was, in essence, "Here it is; react to it."

Not everyone reacted positively. More than a few longtime members, having been schooled by Rabbis Ettelson and Wax in the Classical Reform style of worship, were dismayed by the growing amount of Hebrew in the service and by the trappings of traditional Judaism that the rabbis and some members of the congregation eventually began to wear. One congregant actually resigned when the rabbi began to wear a *tallit*. Danziger handled the objections by trying to minimize the issues. "These are matters of taste, not of principle," he would tell disgruntled congregants. "It's okay not to like them." He also took care never to suggest that the old ways were wrong, and his ways were right. What he *would* say, in carefully chosen, soft-spoken words, is that in his best judgment, the rituals he was introducing were "the right thing for the congregation." In short, he stood his ground.

And so, little by little over the next twenty-two years, Harry Danziger led Temple Israel through what he later described as "an enormous transformation," both in ritual and in style. That he was able to do so with a minimum of conflict was due, at least in part, to his skill in defusing potentially explosive situations. But it was also due, as Danziger himself would be the first to say, to the large reservoir of good will that has always existed in the congregation. "In a lot of places [where there was disagreement over ritual], the rabbi became the issue," he noted. "But at Temple Israel, it was, 'I don't like that, but we're still friends.'"

Early in his tenure, Danziger brought to Temple Israel two individuals who would become closely identified with the congregation's transformation: Barbara Mansberg, who was named director of the religious school in 1980, and John Kaplan, who in 1981 succeeded Michael Weisser (who in turn had succeeded Thomas Schwartz) as the congregation's cantor.

Mansberg, a strong-willed educator with a no-nonsense approach to children and their parents, brought twenty-three years of teaching experience to her new position, but she had no formal training in Jewish education and very little knowledge of Jewish traditions. "My family only lit candles on birthdays," she quipped when asked about her own Jewish upbringing. Nevertheless, she was a quick study — which was fortunate. The religious school had been without a full-time director for several years and

BARBARA MANSBERG
Educational Director, 1980-2001

The Temple Israel Preschool opened in 1988. Among the first students: (CLOCKWISE, FROM FAR LEFT) *Erin Emting, Joel Seligstein, Benjamin Bates, Penny Brucker, Allison Glassick, Molly Evensky, Ashley Glassick, Morgan Montalvo, Jessica Iansmith, Corey Brekher, Brooke Binswanger.*

the congregation's assistant rabbi, Harry Rosenfeld, and teachers Paul Burson and Erma Cohen to adapt the Schuster Curriculum for use in the religious school; they implemented it in kindergarten through sixth grade in just three years. "All kinds of sources were pulled into each lesson," Mansberg recalled. "The teachers felt very comfortable with it, because all the sources were there. And the kids behaved better, because there was something to do."

To enrich the classroom work, Mansberg encouraged dramatic role-playing and even furnished the costumes. For a lesson on Joseph, for example, she provided each third grade class with its own coat of many colors, custom-made for the occasion by Shirley Feibelman. As time went on she scheduled music sessions for every grade, every week — "I had Cantor Kaplan running from one end of the building to another," she confessed, laughing — and she created art projects and put them in kits, so that all the materials a teacher would need, including detailed instructions, were assembled ahead of time. Along the way Mansberg discovered her advance preparation made it easier to recruit teachers — and in particular, substitute teachers — because "they didn't have to worry on Saturday night what they were going to do in class the next morning."

needed a major overhaul. "The curriculum consisted of textbooks and their tables of contents," Mansberg recalled. "Whatever the tables of contents dictated, that's what the children got."

Determined to "bring the Temple religious school into the twentieth century," as she put it, Mansberg read everything she could get her hands on pertaining to Jewish education and began attending the annual meetings of the Conference on Alternatives in Jewish Education (CAJE). At the suggestion of congregant Pat Burnham, she also got in touch with Rabbi Howard Bogot at the New York offices of the Union of American Hebrew Congregations, who acquainted her with what has come to be known as the Schuster Curriculum. "There were no textbooks, and everything was interactive and alive," Mansberg said. "I was thrilled by it."

With Danziger's approval, she began working with

Mansberg, who taught herself to read Hebrew when she began working at Temple and later studied the language at the University of Memphis, eventually expanded the religious school's Hebrew program to every grade, beginning with kindergarten. As part of the curriculum she also familiarized the children with

Jewish traditions, such as kosher food restrictions, that were, in her words, "unconventional for Temple." The goal, she would say later, was "not to promote a revolution, but just to make the children feel comfortable with what some Jews do." She also highlighted the importance of helping others — in the lower grades by using the children's weekly contributions to *Tzedakah* as an opportunity to talk about the importance of meeting human needs, and in the ninth and tenth grades by requiring students to dedicate a certain number of hours each year to community service through a program called *Gemilut Chasadim*. It was largely because of the latter program, organized and supervised by Judy Royal and Roslyn Hirsch, that United Cerebral Palsy in 1988 named Temple Israel "Volunteer Group of the Year."

Within a few years, Mansberg's educational innovations began attracting national recognition. In 1986, the Accreditation Committee of the National Association of Temple Educators rated the religious school "outstanding," and Rabbi Danziger reported to the Board that Temple Israel was now considered one of the centers of excellence in religious education in the Reform Movement.

Mansberg also served as director of the Temple Israel Preschool, which opened in September 1988 over the objections of some members of the Board who feared it would develop into a fullfledged day school. Fifteen years earlier, around the time that courtordered busing was implemented in the Memphis City Schools, the Temple Board had, in fact, looked into the possibility of sponsoring a day school, but the idea never went very far, partly because it encountered strong opposition from members who felt Temple Israel needed to support the public school system, not abandon it. But under the leadership of Mildred Schwartz, the congregation's first female president, most Board members came to see the preschool as a natural and desirable outgrowth of the Sisterhood's successful Mother's Day Out program. "I felt that Temple Israel should be a place where children would be comfortable," Schwartz would say later, "and the best way to make them comfortable was to start them here as young as possible, and then keep them here until they were ready for first grade."

Once the preschool opened, the Temple became a weekday destination for parents, as well. After dropping off their children, many parents stayed on or came back early to help with projects and attend committee meetings. Soon a support group for the school, called Temple Israel Preschool Parents (TIPPS), was organized under the leadership of Susan Edelman, and it provided even more ways for young families to connect with Temple activities. "Previously the building was largely empty during the week," Mansberg noted, "but once the preschool opened, there were people in the Temple all day, every day."

Meanwhile, Cantor John Kaplan was playing his own part in changing the atmosphere at Temple Israel. Arriving at Temple in 1981, he was charged by Danziger with a twofold

JOHN KAPLAN
Cantor of Temple Israel, 1981-

mission: to encourage congregational singing and to bring a sense of joy and warmth to the worship service, all within the framework of the formal ritual. Kaplan had no trouble fulfilling the second part of that mission; his infectious smile and enthusiastic demeanor radiated warmth and joy to the congregation even before he sang the first note. As for the congregation's participation in singing . . . well, that took a little time. Nevertheless, there were hopeful signs right from the start. "The congregation was responding when I first got here," Kaplan recalled. "They may not have been singing, but they were smiling."

Incorporating some of the lively Jewish melodies that Temple youngsters were learning to sing at the Jacobs camp, Kaplan began, with Danziger's approval, using a guitar for accompaniment during services. To a congregation accustomed to hearing the stately tones of an organ during its worship services, the informality of the guitar was a radical — and to some, a jarring — innovation. Nevertheless, like so many other changes

during the Danziger years, the guitar soon became a familiar presence at Temple's services, and as time went on Kaplan occasionally added violins, cellos, flutes, and other instruments to the musical mix, especially on Yom Kippur.

Adult education also flourished under Danziger's leadership — so much so that in 1981 the Temple had to purchase twelve additional six-foot-long tables just to accommodate the scores of members who were turning out to study with the rabbis. The following year President Leo Bearman, Jr., who had been a popular teacher in the religious school ever since he returned to Memphis from law school in 1960, began leading adult students through an exploration of literature relevant to Jews. Twenty-two years later, Bearman's literature course would still be drawing a loyal and enthusiastic crowd. The Lifetime Learning Fund, established by Julian Hohenberg and Honey and Rudi Scheidt, Sr., further enriched the congregation's program offerings during this period, enabling

IRVIN BOGATIN
Congregation President, 1977-1979

LEO BEARMAN, JR.
Congregation President, 1979-1982

SAM HASPEL, JR.
Congregation President, 1982-1984

Temple Israel to bring in guest speakers of the caliber of future Nobel laureate Elie Wiesel (1984) and best-selling novelist Leon Uris (1989).

Congregants even started attending adult Hebrew classes during the 1980s, and a few, having grown up at a time when bar/bat mitzvahs were out of favor in Reform Judaism, decided it was never too late to fulfill the necessary requirements. Hebrew teachers Aileen Ruben and Marcia Levy led the way in this regard; after years of helping to prepare the congregation's children for their bar/bat mitzvahs, the two women belatedly celebrated their own bat mitzvahs at Temple in individual Thursday-morning ceremonies. Later, in 1986, the members of Temple Israel's first adult bar/bat mitzvah class participated in a joint ceremony during Friday night services.

As the activity level at Temple increased during the 1980s, so too did the size of the congregation. By the end of the decade, Temple Israel was serving more than seventeen hundred families. While Danziger welcomed the growth, he soon began warning the officers and trustees of Temple that the congregation's available resources — clergy, space, funds — were being stretched to the limit. Cantor Kaplan, for example, whose duties included helping bar/bat mitzvah candidates learn their assigned Torah portions, found himself by 1988 working with nearly fifty youngsters a year, and the Ritual Committee and clergy were trying to figure out how to schedule such a large number of ceremonies. After considering a variety of alternatives, such as allowing bar/bat mitzvahs to take place during the brief Saturday evening *Havdalah* service that marks the end of *Shabbat*, the Board voted to require all bar/bat mitzvahs to take place on Saturday mornings, even if that meant some youngsters would have to share the special occasion with a classmate.

As in the past, a series of young men filled the position of assistant rabbi during Danziger's tenure, including Alan Greenbaum (1977-81), Harry Rosenfeld (1981-84), Marc Belgrad (1986-91), and Micah Greenstein (1991-). But in 1984 the congregation departed from the norm and hired its first female rabbi: Constance Abramson

CONSTANCE ABRAMSON GOLDEN
Assistant Rabbi, 1984-1986

(later Constance Golden), a forty-one-year-old former casting director for television, stage, and educational films who had trained for the rabbinate at the New York campus of Hebrew Union College-Jewish Institute of Religion.

She was welcomed "very warmly" by the congregation, Golden recalled, even though, to her chagrin, during her first jittery appearance at services she referred to then-President H. Kirke Lewis as "Keith" when she thanked him for the gracious introduction he had just given her. "Kirke never mentioned it, but I was mortified," Golden said, laughing about the embarrassing incident many years later. "They don't teach you in rabbinical school to insult the president of the congregation!"

Having been warned by friends and colleagues that she might encounter a certain amount of resistance from the congregation, Golden was relieved to experience nothing of the kind when she arrived in Memphis. "People were courteous, respectful of me as a rabbi, polite," she recalled. "Nobody patted me on the head and called me 'dear.'" One Sunday afternoon during her first year with the congregation, all the other rabbis in town came to Temple Israel for a community-wide rally in support of Ethiopian Jewry. To her surprise, Golden said, even the Orthodox rabbis "treated me as a colleague."

Still, Temple Israel's first female rabbi did stir up a bit of controversy following her marriage to congregant Dr. Gerald Golden in January 1986. It was not that the marriage of the assistant rabbi to a member of the congregation was an unusual event at Temple Israel. In 1965, at the end of his own first year as assistant rabbi, Danziger himself had married congregant Jeanne Chaban, and more recently Jordan Parr, who served as a rabbinic intern in 1983-84, had married Temple member Cynthia Weiss. (Later on, two other members of the rabbinic staff would wind up standing under a *chuppah* with a bride from Memphis: Rabbi Marc Belgrad with Susan Glazer, and rabbinic intern Seth Stander with Margot Trisch.)

What set tongues wagging in Golden's case was that, as a consequence of her marriage, she decided to leave the full-time rabbinate at the end of her second year with the congregation. Actually, it was Danziger who took the brunt of the ribbing. "He got the business from all those people who said, 'This is what happens when you hire a woman,'" Golden recalled. "I felt guilty and very bad."

For his part, Danziger remembered the situation in somewhat softer tones. "When Connie chose not to continue, I think my feeling and that of others was more disappointment than a sense that this is what happens with women," he said. "In later years, though, I've told Connie that seeing her and Jerry so happy, I apologize for any disapproval I voiced."

Golden and her husband, a pediatric neurologist then associated with the University of Tennessee, stayed on in Memphis for six more years, during which she taught fifth grade at the Temple religious school ("Barbara Mansberg taught me *so* much about teach-

ing!" she recalled), became active in the Sisterhood (Doris Kiersky trained her to transcribe Braille as part of a longtime Sisterhood project), and served as a part-time rabbi for congregations in Meridian, Mississippi, and Blytheville, Arkansas.

In the meantime, Temple Israel — which needed but could not afford a third full-time rabbi — began to supplement its rabbinic staff with students from Hebrew Union College. In addition to Jordan Parr and Seth Stander, five other rabbinic students served one-year internships with the congregation during the 1980s and '90s: Lucy Dinner, Scott Gurdin, Jennifer Weiner, Barry Cohen (who had grown up at Temple Israel), and Eric Stark. Given the increasing demands on the full-time clergy, the interns provided much-needed help with day-to-day pastoral duties.

For the first nine years of his tenure, Danziger also enjoyed the day-to-day support of Joe Boston, Temple Israel's veteran executive director, with whom he shared a congenial and productive partnership. "They functioned as two equal CEOs," noted former president H. Kirke Lewis, whose father, Henry J. Lewis, had been Temple Israel's executive director some twenty years earlier. "Joe managed the building and handled the administrative affairs so efficiently, it left the rabbi free to concentrate all his energy on congregational matters." A stickler for detail, Boston had a standing appointment

JOE BOSTON
Executive Director, 1965-1987

every Friday afternoon to tour the entire building with Mary Whites, the congregation's longtime facilities manager. Together they checked on everything from the wine on the *bimah* to the plumbing in the restrooms. He also was adept at managing the congregation's finances. Many a Temple leader recalled occasions when Boston miraculously found money in the budget to meet some unanticipated, unbudgeted need.

When Boston left Temple Israel in 1987 after twenty-two years with the congregation, "he had a lot of information in his head that wasn't written down," recalled Mildred Schwartz, who was president at the time. In the wake of Boston's departure, the position of executive director turned over four times in the next thirteen years before Jeff Manis took on the congregation's top administrative post in 2000.

Meanwhile, under Danziger's leadership the congregation's volunteer activities were growing more dynamic, and more purposeful, than ever. In response to his Rosh Hashanah sermon in 1983, in which he challenged the members of Temple Israel to "bring life where there is only existence," more than two hundred volunteers signed up to participate in what Danziger called "God's Unfinished Business," a committee that provided help and companionship — a friendly phone call, a thoughtful note, a ride to a doctor's office, a home-cooked meal — to fellow members in need. Coordinated for the first several years by Deanna Kaminsky, the God's Unfinished Business project would still be making a difference in people's lives two decades later.

Around the same time, Murray Reiter, chairman of the Cemetery Committee, volunteered to fill a different type of congregational need. Having determined that the congregation's burial ground was badly in need of attention, Reiter convinced the Board in 1989 to appropriate funds for a long list of improvements;

Temple members Bob Drake (LEFT) and Steve Mendelsohn, repairing monuments at the cemetery in 1990.

then he supervised the project as though he were beautifying his own back yard. Projecting that the cemetery, then more than one hundred years old, would soon run out of space, Reiter and his committee surveyed the members to determine their wishes regarding the location of additional burial plots. Opinion was almost evenly split on the matter — 34 percent preferred to buy more land on Hernando, 32 percent preferred an East Memphis location, and 29 percent had no preference — so in 1991 the Board purchased an additional 1.3 acres on Person Avenue, across from the Temple's existing cemetery. Burials in the new section began in 1994 with the death of Natalya Koshainaya, who had come to the United States from the Soviet Union fourteen years earlier. (During the 1990s, Temple Israel, together with the rest of the Memphis Jewish community, would help to resettle more than three hundred additional Jewish

H. KIRKE LEWIS
Congregation President, 1984-1986

MILDRED SCHWARTZ
Congregation President, 1986-1988

ARTHUR B. "TIM" MALKIN
Congregation President, 1988-1990

immigrants from the former Soviet Union.)

Other volunteer efforts initiated during Danziger's tenure benefited the community at large. Worshippers arriving for Rosh Hashanah services in 1987 found empty grocery bags on all the seats in the sanctuary, along with a request by the Social Justice Committee to fill the bags with canned goods and return them to Temple a few weeks later, in time for the harvest festival of Sukkot. Thus began the congregation's tradition of annual food drives — and later, fund drives — to benefit the Memphis Food Bank. A year later Temple also became a partner in MAZON, the American Jewish organization created to respond to the needs of the hungry.

A number of Temple members ventured into city politics during this period. Dr. Thomas Stern and Bert Prosterman (later Bert Adler Wolff) won election to the Memphis City School Board for the term beginning in 1980, following in the footsteps of Jane Seessel, who had served as an appointee to the board during the 1960s and '70s. (Yet another congregant, Deni Hirsh, would

win a seat on the school board in 2002.) Around the same time, Jeff Sanford became the second Temple member in less than twenty years to be elected to the Memphis City Council; the first, elected in 1966, was Philip Perel.

Meanwhile, Erma Cohen, who had served the congregation in a wide array of volunteer positions over the years, became Temple Israel's first full-time program director in 1992, enabling the congregation to take on a number of ambitious, labor-intensive projects that were previously beyond its scope. In 1994, led by Linda S. Kaplan, Marjean Kremer, and Selma Lewis, the congregation joined with members of the Lutheran community to build a house for Habitat for Humanity. And in April 1998 the congregation went all out for its first Mitzvah Day. Underwritten by a fund established by Mickey and Warren Wurzburg, Sr., and chaired by Arlyne Schwartz, Temple Israel's first Mitzvah Day involved more than nine hundred volunteers — men, women, and children — who fanned out across the city to repair homes, serve food at a homeless shelter, plant flowers at a nursing home, clean up a cemetery, and put their talents to work on seventy other community-service projects. The success of the first Mitzvah Day guaranteed it would be repeated the following year, and every year after that, continuing into the twenty-first century.

At least part of the congregation's increased activity level during the 1980s and '90s stemmed from a 1983 report by the Long Range Planning Committee, chaired by Jocelyn Rudner, which had recommended, among other things, that Temple Israel find more ways to involve its members in the life of the congregation. One way to do this was to create more opportunities for members to serve in leadership positions, so the congregation approved a series of bylaw changes in 1983 and 1985 that established term limits for its officers and trustees. Under the new provisions, Temple Israel's president and senior vice president were limited to two consecutive one-year terms in

office, and Board members were limited to two consecutive two-year terms.

So it was that during Danziger's twenty-two years as senior rabbi, Temple Israel elected no fewer than eleven different presidents: Irvin Bogatin; Leo Bearman, Jr.; Sam Haspel, Jr.; H. Kirke Lewis; Mildred S. Schwartz; Arthur B. "Tim" Malkin; Neil E. "Nick" Ringel; James B. Jalenak; Rudi E. Scheidt, Sr.; Judith E. Royal; and Benjamin Isenberg. Of these, Bearman, who led the congregation from 1979-82, was the only president to hold the office for more than two years, and he was the last one eligible to do so.

From Bogatin to Isenberg, every president during the Danziger years wound up wrestling with the budget, struggling to bring the congregation's income, which came primarily from dues, into line with its rapidly growing expenses. For a while, Abe Plough quietly funded the operating deficits, making gifts of $20,000, $30,000, and even $60,000 to bridge the

NEIL E. "NICK" RINGEL
Congregation President, 1990-1992

JAMES B. JALENAK
Congregation President, 1992-1994

RUDI E. SCHEIDT, SR.
Congregation President, 1994-1996

gap between income and expenses. The congregation became so dependent on Plough's generosity that when Bearman became president, he was led to believe, he recalled, that the way to balance the budget at the end of the fiscal year was simply "to go over there [to Plough's office at Poplar and Perkins] and talk for a little bit and chat about this and that, and then Mr. Plough would say, 'Well, what do you need?' and you'd tell him, and then he would pick up the deficit."

Thus in the summer of 1979, President Leo Bearman, Jr., and Executive Director Joe Boston went together to pay a call on Abe Plough. Bearman, just forty-four years old at the time, got down to business with the formidable octogenarian — by then, virtually a legend in his own time — as quickly as he dared. "We've got this deficit, Mr. Plough," he began. But this time the congregation's longtime benefactor didn't reach for his checkbook. Instead, he looked straight at the congregation's president and executive director and said, "Well, then *you'd* better get to work!" And that was that. Meeting adjourned.

Stunned, Bearman and Boston retreated to the hall outside Plough's office and tried to figure out what they had done wrong. "I don't mind telling you I was scared," Bearman admitted years later. "We came back to Temple and turned off every third light in the administrative wing to save electricity, and after that we started closing the building on Mondays to cut costs."

Ultimately, Plough did erase the deficit again that year — without fanfare, as always, and only after the Board's economy measures reduced the shortfall by 17 percent. Then, in 1980, he went a step further: he established a $100,000 Perpetual Endowment Fund, stipulating that the money was to be invested only in AA or AAA bonds or certificates of deposit.

Two years later, Plough, then ninety-one years old and still vitally interested in the growth and financial security of the congregation, spearheaded a campaign to boost the Endowment Fund's assets to $2 million. A campaign committee was formed, and at one of its early meetings in Plough's office, Nick Ringel, then a relative rookie as a Temple officer, challenged Plough's assumption that the drive could be conducted primarily by phone and by mail. That kind of money, Ringel ventured, could only be raised through face-to-face solicitations. "What's your name?" Plough asked abruptly, staring hard at this outspoken newcomer. "Nick Ringel, sir," the newcomer replied. "Well, Mr. Ringel," Plough said, "you've just become chairman of this committee."

Leaving Plough's office after the meeting, Ringel and his newly appointed co-chairs, Larry Lewis and Tim Malkin, solicited each other's contributions while riding the elevator to the ground floor, and under their leadership the Endowment Committee went on to raise $1 million over the next year. Later, Sam Cooper, who had recently retired from HumKo, took over the chairmanship and completed the task. In January 1986 Cooper announced the Perpetual Endowment Fund had reached its revised goal of $2.5 million, and the Board voted to have the names of everyone who contributed to the campaign etched on glass panels that would be mounted on the wall across from the Gift Shop.

Plough himself did not live to see the Endowment Fund reach its goal; the congregation's honorary president, who was celebrated not only for his business acumen, but also for his extraordinary generosity to charitable organizations in Memphis and across the country, died in September 1984 at the age of ninety-two. After Plough's death, the position of honorary president of Temple Israel was left vacant until 1993, when the congregation awarded that distinction to the man with whom Plough had worked so closely over the years to fulfill their mutual goals for the Temple —

Sam Cooper. Cooper remained honorary president until his death in 1999.

Meanwhile, even with the additional income provided by the Perpetual Endowment Fund, the task of balancing the budget grew more and more difficult as the years passed. In 1986 the Board cut costs by reducing the Temple's newsletter, *The Voice*, from a weekly to a bi-weekly publication, and at various times certain staff positions were left unfilled. But even more effort went into increasing the congregation's income. All manner of fund-raisers were held, from a special event billed as The First Annual Lalapalooza Fund-Raising Dinner — which was followed a few years later by the *last* Annual Lalapalooza Fund-Raising Dinner — to a long-term

project, organized by Juliet Klein, called "Grocery Gelt," through which certain local supermarkets donated a percentage of members' purchases to Temple.

Under the guidance of Linda S. Kaplan, Richard Lightman, and Judy Boston, celebrated violinists Itzhak Perlman and Pinchas Zukerman were booked to perform in the Temple sanctuary, thereby expanding the congregation's cultural horizons as well as its coffers. And on a balmy Sunday evening in April 1989, the Memphis Symphony Orchestra presented a pops concert on the Temple grounds. An immediate crowd-pleaser, the pops concert — later moved to Mother's Day and dubbed "Moms and Pops" — went on to become an annual springtime event at Temple Israel.

Members and guests singing the national anthem at the "Moms and Pops" concert, May 2004.

By far the most ambitious and successful fund-raising project staged by the congregation during this period was the series of "Way Off Broadway" shows that began in 1990. The first show, chaired by Fran and Jeff Winstock, made a profit of $47,000, and later productions netted even more. Meanwhile, the proceeds of the Brotherhood's annual auctions and Sisterhood's Holland bulb sales were used to subsidize activities that were not covered by the Temple's overall budget.

Still, financial problems continued to plague the congregation throughout the 1980s and '90s. Faced with increasing costs and a growing demand for more programs and services, especially for the congregation's youth, the Temple's leadership conducted numerous campaigns to persuade members to increase their dues, or their "annual commitment," as congregants' yearly contributions to Temple came to be known. But in spite of these efforts, during the last two decades of the twentieth century the congregation's yearly financial predicament — insufficient income to meet its operating expenses — became a chronic condition.

In 1996 congregation President Rudi Scheidt, Sr., seeing no end to the annual budget deficits that were keeping many a Temple leader awake at night, told the Executive Committee he thought the time had come to consider a major capital and endowment campaign to ensure the financial stability of the congregation. Six more years — and six more budget crises — would pass before such a campaign would get underway.

FRAN AND JEFF WINSTOCK
Co-chairs of the first three "Way Off Broadway" productions

"The three most important criteria for beginning your rabbinate in a large pulpit," Rabbi Micah D. Greenstein once said, paraphrasing an old joke about real estate, "are senior rabbi, senior rabbi, senior rabbi."

MICAH GREENSTEIN
*Spiritual leader of
Temple Israel, 2000-*

For Greenstein, that quip was more than just a clever bit of conventional wisdom. In the spring of 1991, when he was looking for a favorable place to begin his own rabbinic career, it was the guiding principle that led him to Harry Danziger's congregation in Memphis, Tennessee. "I saw Harry as a balanced mentor, and as a great rabbi to work with and learn from," Greenstein, then twenty-eight, recalled. In addition, he said, Dr. Jacob Rader Marcus, his adviser at Hebrew Union College-Jewish Institute of Religion (HUC-JIR) in Cincinnati, had spoken highly of Temple Israel, assuring him the Reform congregation in Memphis had a long history of "dedicated, loyal, fine" leadership.

For their part, the leaders of Temple Israel were equally taken with Greenstein. His résumé included an impressive list of academic credentials — Bachelor of Arts in Economics from Cornell University; Master of Arts in Public Administration from the John F. Kennedy School of Government at Harvard University; ordination by HUC-JIR in Cincinnati, where he received, among other honors, the same award for "best sermon delivery" that Harry Danziger had won twenty-seven years earlier; and a second Master of Arts in Hebrew Letters from HUC-

JIR in Los Angeles. But beyond his résumé, what the officers and trustees of Temple Israel saw when they met Micah Greenstein for the first time was a young man positively bubbling over with intelligence, charm, and vitality. Greenstein was chosen "not only because of his abilities and intellectual qualities," James B. Jalenak, then vice president of the congregation, recalled, "but especially because of his energy and enthusiasm."

Following the strict rules that governed HUC-JIR's placement system at the time, Harry Danziger telephoned Greenstein at exactly 8 a.m. on the designated day in May 1991 to offer him the position at Temple Israel. Greenstein, who was also being courted by a number of other congregations, accepted the offer from Memphis. Thus, as they say in Yiddish, the *shiddach* was made. Greenstein and his wife, Sheril, whom he had met for the first time at a summer camp for Reform Jewish youth when he was twelve and she was nine, arrived in Memphis in the summer of 1991, and he was installed as the congregation's assistant rabbi in October of that year. His father, Rabbi Howard R. Greenstein, then the spiritual leader of Congregation Ahavath Chesed (otherwise known as The Temple) in Jacksonville, Florida, delivered the sermon at his installation service.

Temple Israel's new young rabbi quickly carved a place for himself in Memphis. Within a few years he was a familiar sight not just on the *bimah* at Temple Israel, but at civic and religious gatherings all over town — as a member of the Executive Board of the National Civil Rights Museum, as an adviser to the city's Race Relations and Diversity Institute, as president of the Memphis Ministers Association, and even as a featured speaker in Calvary Episcopal Church's Lenten

Assistant Rabbi Micah Greenstein leading a Tot Shabbat service.

Series; he was the first rabbi invited to participate in this respected lecture series since its inception seventy-eight years earlier. Along the way Greenstein also found time to co-author with his father the final chapter of a book titled, *The Quiet Voices: Southern Rabbis and Black Civil Rights, 1880s to 1990s*.[100]

At Temple, Greenstein focused his attention at first on the religious school's high school department, where he worked to boost the enrollment and strengthen the curriculum. He also helped design innovative adult programming, such as a one-day crash course in beginning Hebrew, called a "Hebrew Marathon," which he introduced in 1992. And, of course, he tended to the members' spiritual needs, sometimes in unconventional ways. Not long after he arrived, congregants began hearing that Greenstein was bringing calm and comfort to gravely ill patients by singing softly to them at their bedside.

As was the case in many parts of the world, the pace of life at Temple Israel seemed to quicken during the last decade of the twentieth century, and the 1990s passed in a whirlwind of activity: congregational trips to Israel; Confirmation class trips to explore "Jewish New York"; "Tot *Shabbat*" services for families with young children; daily *minyans* for those who wanted to say *Kaddish* for a departed loved one, or who just wanted to pray; preschool graduations; MeFTY conclaves; high-profile guest speakers, such as Pulitzer Prize-winning columnist Thomas Friedman; musical programs by singer/songwriter Debbie Friedman and other contemporary Jewish musicians. The only real pause in the action came in February 1994, when a huge ice storm knocked out most of the city's electrical power, including Temple Israel's. With no heat and no lights and virtually no one willing to brave the icy streets, the congregation canceled its Friday evening worship service for the first and, as far as is known, only time in its history. (An earlier power outage had darkened the Temple building in November 1990, but on that occasion *Shabbat* services were held by candlelight. Danziger reported afterward that some participants enjoyed the service so much, they asked if the cozy "campfire setting" could be repeated.)

In 1993 Herta and Dr. Justin H. Adler donated their large and valuable Judaica collection to the congregation, and Honey and Rudi Scheidt, Sr., funded the construction of a museum for the collection on the second floor of the Temple. Around that same time the congregation received another precious artifact, Holocaust Torah Number 162, which had been discovered after the end of World War II in a warehouse outside Prague. Housed in a display case at Temple, this remnant of a congregation destroyed by the Nazis was brought into the sanctuary for use every year on Simchat Torah, the holiday when Jewish congregations reach the end of their year-long reading of the Torah and then, without pause, scroll all the way back to Genesis and start reading it again. To read from the Holocaust Torah on that particular day, Greenstein later explained, "is to show that just as the cycle of Torah never ends, the Jewish people never end."

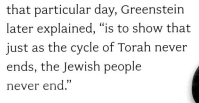

Holocaust Torah Number 162

With a trend toward casual attire sweeping the nation, Temple Israel in 1997 began offering a forty-five minute, come-as-you-are service in the chapel two Friday evenings a month, followed by blessings over the *Shabbat* candles, wine, and challah in the lobby. The warmth and intimacy of the service, combined with its brevity and informality, made the 6:15 p.m. "early service" an instant hit with the members, and in October 1999 it became a weekly event. Two months later, on Friday, December 31, 1999, more than four hundred members of the congregation chose to kick off their celebration of the momentous, turn-of-the-millennium New Year's Eve by attending the early service at Temple Israel.

By the mid-1990s, Micah Greenstein was such an integral part of Temple life that many members had begun to view him as the logical successor to Harry Danziger. With the congregation's

JEANNE AND RABBI HARRY DANZIGER *on the eve of his retirement, May 2000*

wholehearted approval, Greenstein was promoted to associate rabbi in 1994, and over the next five years, as he worked side by side with Danziger, his impact on the congregation and the community continued to grow. In March 1999, when Danziger surprised the congregation by announcing, just four months after his sixtieth birthday, that he intended to retire in September 2000, Greenstein was the obvious — and overwhelming — choice to succeed him. During Danziger's last year as senior rabbi, a twelve-month period that spanned the end of the twentieth century and the beginning of the twenty-first, he and Greenstein worked in tandem, serving as co-rabbis of Temple Israel.

Thus Temple Israel had the good fortune, once again, to experience an extraordinarily smooth transition from one spiritual leader to another. In May of 2000 — or Y2K, as that pivotal year was commonly referred to in turn-of-the-century jargon — a huge crowd of congregants turned out to express their admiration for Danziger and his wife, Jeanne, who had been nearly as active in congregational life as her husband. As a sign of their affection, the members named the Temple's chapel in the Danzigers' honor. (Danziger would be almost as busy in his retirement as he was earlier; in 2003 he was elected vice president of the Central Conference of American Rabbis, with the expectation that he would become president in 2005.) Then, on a Friday night in September 2000, another huge crowd gathered to celebrate the installation of Micah D. Greenstein as the eighth senior rabbi in Temple Israel's history.

The Temple over which Greenstein assumed leadership was in many ways a study in contrasts: more traditional in its approach to Judaism than it had been in nearly a hundred years, it was more innovative, as well. At the dawn of the twenty-first century, Temple

Israel was a synagogue where bar/bat mitzvah ceremonies were customary; where Hebrew was read, chanted, and sung by the congregation as well as the clergy; and where the rabbis and some congregants wore the traditional *yarmulkes* and *tallitot*. But it was also a place where the solemn observance of Yom Kippur included an upbeat *Ruach* service, led by a contemporary music ensemble that included Greenstein himself; where the holiday of Purim was accompanied by a fun-filled (and pun-filled) musical send-up of the Book of Esther called "The Megillah Goes to Woodstock"; where the end of the week-long holiday of Pesach, when Jews customarily abstain from eating bread, was celebrated with a Pizza Fest; and where the old *Union Prayer Book*, slightly modified, was back in use one Friday night a month at a Classical Reform worship service.

With a membership of some eighteen hundred families — a number that exceeded the total membership of the five other local synagogues (four Orthodox, one Conservative) combined — the congregation included more than five thousand men, women, and children in the Memphis area. Its size alone posed a challenge to the rabbinical staff, which by 2001 included not only Greenstein, but also two other full-time rabbis. But even more challenging was the fact that the members of Temple Israel were more scattered geographically, and far more diverse in their religious background and outlook, than ever before.

SHERIL AND RABBI MICAH GREENSTEIN
at his installation as senior rabbi, September 2000

Long gone were the days when everyone at Temple knew everyone else from the time they were children. By the early part of the twenty-first century, the congregation included about 480 families — approximately one-fourth of the total membership — who had joined within the previous ten years. Some had come to Temple by way of Reform congregations in other parts of the country; others had grown up in Conservative or Orthodox congregations, in Memphis or elsewhere; still others had found their way not just to Temple Israel, but to Judaism itself, as adults. "Our congregation is a wonderful hybrid," Greenstein observed. "*K'lal yisrael* is no longer about oneness with 'them.' *K'lal yisrael* has come home to Temple."

Like the rest of the nation's population, Temple Israel's membership was aging. By 2004, nearly 1,500 congregants — close to 38 percent — were over the age of fifty, and more than 210 were over eighty. Still, the Temple's membership also included about 800 children. While earlier generations of Temple Israel's children were generally clustered in a handful of select public and private schools, now the offspring of Temple members attended as many as forty-eight different public schools and twenty-five private schools stretching all the way from DeSoto County, Mississippi, to Collierville. Faced with the dilemma of how to create programming for this scattered population of Jewish young people, the congregation in 2000 hired a full-time youth director. The candidate chosen for the position was a modern-day Pied Piper named Michael Danziger (otherwise known as "Ziggy"), the youngest of Jeanne and Rabbi Harry Danziger's three sons.

More and more, Temple Israel was also being called upon to provide a full range of services to Reform Jews living outside Memphis. While Temple had always served as a focal point for Reform Jewry from the Missouri Boot Heel to the Mississippi Delta, nearly a dozen Jewish communities in the region had maintained their own congregations as well. Now, however, those Jewish communities were shrinking, and the congregations that once served them had resorted to operating on a part-time basis or, like Temple Israel in Blytheville, Arkansas, had shut down entirely. The result: "When a bat mitzvah girl and her family in Cleveland, Mississippi, need a rabbi, Temple Israel [in Memphis] serves that family," Greenstein told his congregation in 2000. "Conversions or weddings in Jackson, Tennessee — *we* have made that possible." In light of the situation, Greenstein began referring to Temple as "a FedEx hub for Judaism in the Mid-South."

In addition to these challenges, the congregation was contending with a host of worries brought on by a new wave of suicide bombings in Israel — and by the horrifying events of September 11, 2001, which shook America to the core. The eve of Rosh Hashanah fell on September 17 in 2001, just six days after the attacks that destroyed the World Trade Center in New York and part of the Pentagon in Washington. Shocked by the size and scope of the terrorist acts and unnerved by the prospect that additional deadly assaults might be forthcoming, the members of Temple Israel gathered to usher in the Jewish New Year under a shadow of gloom and apprehension, more aware than ever of the uncertainties of life. The familiar words of the Rosh Hashanah liturgy, "On Rosh Hashanah it is written and on Yom Kippur it is sealed, who shall live and who shall die, who by fire and who by water . . ." took on added meaning that night, as did that oft-repeated, but suddenly more urgent phrase from the *Avinu Malkeinu*, "Our Father, our King, keep far from our country pestilence, war, and famine."

When it was time for the sermon, Greenstein did not try to make sense of the attacks, or of the tragic loss of life that resulted from them. Looking out at a sea of anxious faces, he focused instead on the extraordinary bravery and kindness shown by some of the victims. He called to the members' attention the last phone calls that so many of the victims made — not to cry out in anguish or bemoan their fate, but simply to say "I love you" to the people nearest and dearest to them. "Those last cell phone calls remind us of the importance of leaving no issue unresolved with our loved ones," Greenstein told the congregation. "They remind us of the fragility of life and the importance of taking nothing for granted, especially the things that matter most — life, love, family, faith.

"My dear friends," Greenstein concluded, "this week has been too much for any of us to bear alone. We need each other and we need God's help. For with God's help, we can hold each other up and help our children, and their children, become the blessings we and they were meant to be. May God hear our prayers on this Rosh Hashanah eve, and may God grant us the resolve and the strength to get through these trying times. Judaism says we can do it. Our people have always found a way. So can we."[101]

By the time of the attacks on September 11, the leaders of Temple Israel were fully engaged in planning the most ambitious capital campaign in the congregation's history. The need for such a campaign had been discussed informally during the presidencies of Judy Royal and Ben Isenberg, but it was the new senior

JUDITH E. ROYAL
Congregation President, 1996-1998

BENJAMIN ISENBERG
Congregation President, 1998-2000

SHERRY SAMUELS
Congregation President, 2000-2002

rabbi who provided the impetus to get it underway. During the ten years he had spent at Temple Greenstein had witnessed the Board's repeated efforts to increase the income from dues, and he had come to realize, as had many of the officers and trustees themselves, that the only permanent solution to the annual budget deficits was to greatly increase the size of the Perpetual Endowment Fund. In the spring of 2000, as he contemplated the challenges he would face as the spiritual leader of Temple Israel, Greenstein concluded that in order for him "to re-invigorate Temple for a new century . . . and create meaningful Jewish experiences and spiritual opportunities for thousands of Jews of all ages," he would "need the resources to make it happen."

Shortly afterward, Greenstein asked former President Nick Ringel to spearhead the organization of a capital campaign to ensure the congregation's future. Ringel started out by enlisting the support of Bob Solmson and Billy Orgel, and later Ira Lipman. Then,

with the help of Kenneth Wurzburg, Mark Halperin, Steve Wishnia, and Sherry Samuels, he assembled a steering committee whose members were so committed to the project, they willingly attended 7:30 a.m. meetings twice a month for more than two years. After much thought, and with what some people considered a heavy dose of blind faith, the committee set the goal for the campaign at the unprecedented level of $25 million. Half the money would be used to remodel and refurbish the Temple building, which was showing the effects of twenty-five years of wear and tear, and the other half would go into the Endowment Fund to help support both program and staffing needs.

Then came September 11. As the stock market plummeted in the aftermath of the attacks, the steering committee began to question the wisdom of going ahead with its ambitious plans. Once again, however, the Plough Foundation provided help at the critical moment. Just as its founder, Abe Plough, had led the way a generation earlier when the congregation's dream was to build a new Temple, the Plough Foundation gave this new capital campaign an all-important head start: a $5 million commitment to the drive on the front end, and the promise of an additional $3 million grant if and when the total amount of pledges reached $22 million.

With this kind of encouragement, the committee forged ahead in spite of the weak business climate, and the response was overwhelmingly positive. More than two hundred Temple members signed up to work on the campaign — more than twice the number of volunteer solicitors a professional fund-raiser had suggested would be needed — and by the beginning of 2004, the ambitious $25 million goal, the largest

fund-raising initiative in the history of the Memphis Jewish community, was reached. "The name of this campaign, 'A Gift for Generations,' really did signify what the effort was all about," congregation President Kenneth Wurzburg noted as the drive reached its successful conclusion. "Through their generosity, the current generation of Temple members have ensured the stability of the congregation for generations to come."

And so Temple

A Gift for Generations

THE GIFT FOR GENERATIONS CAMPAIGN "BREAKFAST-CLUBBERS"
SEATED: (LEFT TO RIGHT) *Bob Solmson, Steve Wishnia, Nick Ringel, Judy Royal, Juliet Klein.* STANDING: *Kenneth Wurzburg, Jerrold Graber, Billy Orgel , Rabbi Micah Greenstein, Executive Director Jeff Manis, Lee Filderman, Campaign Administrator Marilyn Schachter, Mark Halperin. Not pictured: Dr. Thom Lobe, Sherry Samuels.*

Architectural rendering of the planned renovation/addition to Temple Israel

Israel reached its 150th year, spiritually vibrant, financially secure, and, despite the challenges inherent in meeting the needs of more than four thousand individuals, committed to facing the future as one congregation. A "wonderful hybrid," as its rabbi described it, Temple Israel at 150 was open to fresh ideas as well as time-honored traditions, first-generation members as well as longtime loyalists who remembered how things were done at Temple "way back when." Even its leadership reflected this harmonious blend of new and old. Two of Temple's most recent presidents, Ben Isenberg and Sherry Samuels, were transplants to Memphis who had joined Temple Israel as adults, while the two who succeeded them, Kenneth Wurzburg and Mark Halperin, had deep roots at Temple. Wurzburg's grandfather, Abe Wurzburg, had led the congregation in the 1940s; Halperin's father, Lawrence Halperin, had served as president not only of the Temple Israel Brotherhood, but also of the National Federation of Temple Brotherhoods, in the 1970s.

Under Greenstein's leadership, Temple Israel had a new team of professional educators in place by the time of its 150th anniversary. Following Barbara Mansberg's retirement in 2001, Susan Feld, a specialist in early childhood education, was named director of the preschool, and a year later Barb Zelonky was recruited from California to serve as director of education. As part of a new, comprehensive approach to lifetime learning at Temple, Zelonky would supervise not only the religious school, but also the full range of adult educational courses that were continuing to grow in number and popularity. Another important staff change came in 2004, when the congregation hired its first husband-and-wife rabbinic team, Meir and Tara Feldman, to succeed the two previous associate rabbis, Valerie Cohen and Daniel Rabishaw.

KENNETH WURZBURG
Congregation President, 2002-2004

MARK HALPERIN
Congregation President, 2004 -

Three special events were held in 2003-04 to mark the congregation's sesquicentennial anniversary. The first, chaired by Harriet and Dr. Tom Stern, celebrated Temple Israel's rich history with a congregational dinner, an exhibit of historic photographs and artifacts put together by the Temple's archivist, Linde Feibelman, and three guest speakers — Bill Ettelson, Jonathan Wax, and Jeffrey Danziger — who reminisced about what it was like to grow up at Temple as "the rabbi's kid." The second event, chaired by Mary Lynn and Arnold Perl, brought to Temple an array of Memphis's religious, civic, and political leaders who highlighted the congregation's 150-year partnership with the larger community. The finale to the year-long celebration came in May 2004, when the congregation assembled for its 150th annual meeting, chaired by Peggy and Lenny Goodman. Rabbi Eric H. Yoffie, president of the Union for Reform Judaism (formerly

CO-CHAIRS OF TEMPLE ISRAEL'S 150TH ANNIVERSARY EVENTS
(LEFT TO RIGHT) *Arnold and Mary Lynn Perl, Dr. Tom and Harriet Stern, Peggy and Lenny Goodman*

the Union of American Hebrew Congregations), was the evening's guest speaker.

Ironically, Temple Israel's exciting anniversary year had started out on a distinctly inauspicious note. In July 2003, just as the various committees were making arrangements for the sesquicentennial events, a ferocious, hundred-mile-per-hour windstorm blew through Memphis, snapping utility poles, smashing windows, tearing roofs off homes and businesses, and toppling thousands of huge trees. On the heavily wooded Temple property, destruction and debris were everywhere: one giant oak had landed on the Noah's Ark building, another had fallen against the main building, and nearly a hundred other trees were strewn on the ground like Pik-Up-Stix.

At *Shabbat* services three days later — which drew a sizeable crowd, even though most of the city, including Temple Israel, was still functioning without electricity — Greenstein commented on an observation he had made while surveying the damage. The trees that were toppled by the wind, he said, were the ones that had been standing alone. The trees that survived were the ones that were standing close together, with their roots intertwined.

It was a perfect metaphor for the congregation itself. Ultimately, the source of Temple Israel's enduring strength was not its style of worship, or its large membership, or its imposing building; it was, in essence, what Harry Danziger had recognized the first time he came to town — that the congregation was a true partnership between its rabbis and its members.

Over the course of 150 years, Temple Israel had survived and flourished because its members and rabbis had stood together, side by side, through all the joys and vicissitudes that came their way. United in a common purpose and connected by a shared vision, they had weathered life's storms because their roots — and their futures — were intertwined.

May 2004: The congregation gathered in the Ettelson-Wax Hall for its 150th annual meeting.

Presidents of Temple Israel's Auxiliary Organizations

SISTERHOOD

ADALIN BARNETT
JOY BEARMAN
JUDY BEARMAN
HATTIE BLOCK
MARY BRONSTEIN
PAT BURNHAM
ERMA COHEN
IRENE COHEN
BONNIE COOPER
DOROTHY DAVIS
GERTRUDE DELUGACH
BETTY DLUGACH
JANE ECKSTEIN
NELL ETTELSON
SHIRLEY FEIBELMAN
RAY GATTMAN
RANA GOODMAN
EFFIE GREENER
MILDRED HAAS
JANE HARMEL
GERRY HASPEL
HORTENSE JACOBS
MARY LOVE KASSELBERG
DOROTHY KLEIN
LYNN KLINE
MRS. HARRY LEWIS
DEBBIE OGNIBENE
BARBARA OSTROW
IDE PERLBERG
SHELLY PIERCE
SUSAN LEVIT PLOUGH
EDITH REITER
LEONA ROSEN
MATTIE ROSENFIELD

HERMOISE ROTH
JUDY ROYAL
JOCELYN RUDNER
LAVERNE SIEGEL
HAZEL SUMMERFIELD
EILEEN WISHNIA
DAISY WOLFF
LYN YUKON

BROTHERHOOD

CHARLES AUERBACH
LEO BEARMAN, JR.
HERBERT BENHAM, JR.
NEAL BERLIN
I.M. BILSKY
MILTON BINSWANGER, JR.
IRVIN BOGATIN
COLMAN BOROWSKY
A.C. BURNHAM
VICTOR BUTCHER
ALLEN COHEN
I. STANLEY COOPER
ROBERT DRAKE
HERSCHEL FEIBELMAN
NATHAN FEIBELMAN
JAKE FENBERG
SIDNEY A. FEUERSTEIN
DR. IRVING FILDERMAN
ARTHUR FRIEDMAN
BENJAMIN GOODMAN, JR.
FRED GRAFLUND
DANIEL GREIF
LESLIE GRUBER
JOSEPH HAAS
RONALD HAAS

LAWRENCE HALPERIN
SIGMUND HILLER
BRUCE KAHN
PHILIP KAMINSKY
ROBERT KREMER
SCOT LANSKY
ARTHUR LETTES
SUMNER LEVINE
DR. LOUIS LEVY
SANFORD LICHTERMAN
ARTHUR MALKIN
BRUCE MINKOFF
MAX NOTOWITZ
BILLY ORGEL
RICHARD ORGEL
FRANK PIERCE
HARVEY PIERCE
MURRAY REITER
ALVIN SALOMON
EARLE SCHWARZ
JEFFREY WINSTOCK
RICHARD WOLF

JUNIOR CONGREGATION/ MEMPHIS FEDERATION OF TEMPLE YOUTH

LARRY ADLER
MISSY ALPERT
SEAN ALPERT
BETSY BARNETT
STANLEY BASSIST
ELAINE BEARMAN
LEO BEARMAN, JR.
RACHEL BEARMAN
CAROLINE BERZ

CAROLINE BILLER
EMMA SUE BINSWANGER
MAXINE BLECKER
LYDIA BLOOM
JULIE BURNHAM
FELIX CALDWELL
JERRY CALDWELL
JEFF CHUTZ
BARRY COHEN
BRETT COHEN
MICHAEL DANZIGER
SHELBY DEENEY
DON DELUGACH
HARRY DELUGACH
LOUIS EDELSON
MICHAEL EDELSON
HARRIET FEIBELMAN
JEF FEIBELMAN
DAVID FELSENTHAL
EDDIE FELSENTHAL
ARTHUR H. FRIEDMAN
DANIEL GREIF
I.G. GOLDSMITH
J.B. HEYMAN, JR.
SIGMUND HILLER, JR.
ROGER HIRSCH
JAMES B. JALENAK
ALLYN KANTOR
HUBERT KIERSKY
ROBERT KLINE
HENRY LEVY
JOE LEVY
ERMA LEWIS
TIFFANY LOEWENBERG
JOSEPH MAUREY
TAMARA MAUREY

RONALD MOSKOVITZ
JANET PACHTER
MICHAEL PAHN
ROLAND PAUL, JR.
SCOTT PRICE
JIMMY RINGEL
DAVID ROSENTHAL
ELISA ROSENTHAL
NATALIE ROYAL
IRA SACHS, JR.
RANDY SALKY
ALFRED SCHARFF
ELIZABETH SCHARFF
NANCY SCHNEIDER
ANNA SCHWARZ
EARLE SCHWARZ
JAY SCHWARZ
MARVIN SHINBAUM
COLE SILVERMAN
BRAD SNYDER
ELLEN SNYDER
STEVE SNYDER
JOE STUART
LISA USDAN
FRED VOSSE
M.J. VOSSE, JR.
FRIEDA WAINMAN
JONATHAN WAX
CYNTHIA WEISS

Glossary of Hebrew Terms

bar or bat mitzvah. *A son or daughter of the commandment; the ceremony marking the initiation of a child into the Jewish religious community and into the observance of the precepts of the Torah.*

Barechu. *The call to worship: "Praise God, to Whom our praise is due!"*

bimah. *The altar in a synagogue; site of the ark that holds one or more Torahs.*

bris or brit. *Literally, a covenant. Bris/brit milah means "the covenant of circumcision"; bris is often used as a short form of bris/brit milah.*

Chanukah. *The eight-day Festival of Lights, which commemorates the Maccabees' victory over the Greek rulers of Syria and the rededication of the Temple in Jerusalem in 165 B.C.E.*

chazan. *A cantor.*

chuppah. *A wedding canopy.*

Ein Keiloheinu. *"There is none like our God," a well-known hymn sung on the Sabbath and festivals in Jewish liturgy.*

gemilut chasadim. *Acts of loving kindness.*

High Holy Days. *The period of ten days each fall that begins with Rosh Hashanah, the Jewish New Year, and concludes with Yom Kippur, the Day of Atonement.*

Kaddish. *A sanctification of God's name that has five different forms; the most well-known form is the "mourner's kaddish" recited by mourners at the end of a worship service.*

k'lal Yisrael. *A feeling of oneness with all other Jews.*

minyan. *Ten adult Jews (in Orthodox Judaism, ten adult men), the minimum number required to conduct a worship service.*

Pesach. *The festival of Passover, which commemorates the liberation of the Israelites from slavery and their exodus from Egypt.*

Purim. *The holiday that falls in the Hebrew month of Adar (February-March), on which the Megillah, the story of Esther, is read.*

Rosh Hashanah. *The Jewish New Year, which ushers in a ten-day period of prayer and repentance that culminates with Yom Kippur.*

ruach. *Spirit.*

Shabbos or Shabbat. *The Jewish Sabbath, observed from sundown on Friday until Saturday evening. The day is marked by prayer, rest, and enjoyment.*

Shavuot. *The spring holiday that commemorates the revelation at Mount Sinai and the receiving of the Ten Commandments.*

Shema. *The watchword of the Jewish faith from Deuteronomy 6:4: "Hear, O Israel: the Eternal is our God, the Eternal is One."*

shiddach *(Yiddish). A marital match.*

shochet. *A ritual slaughterer trained in the regulations governing the Jewish dietary laws.*

sukkah. *An outdoor structure that is left open to the stars; used for dining during Sukkot (see below).*

Sukkot. *The autumn harvest festival that commemorates the wandering of the Israelites through the wilderness; during Sukkot it is customary to dine outdoors in a sukkah.*

tallis or tallit. *A prayer shawl. In the Sephardic dialect (tallit), the plural is tallitot.*

Talmud. *The name applied to the collection of rabbinic discussions of Jewish law between 200-500 C.E. The Talmud consists of the Mishnah and the Gemara.*

Torah. *In its narrow meaning, the Five Books of Moses, written on a parchment scroll. It is also known as the "Written Law."*

tzedakah. *Righteousness; charity.*

Vaanachnu. *The last part of the Aleinu, or concluding prayer of "Adoration": "We bow our heads in reverence before the Eternal God, the Holy One, blessed be God."*

yad. *Literally, a hand; refers to a pointer that is used when reading the Torah.*

yahrtzeit. *Literally, a year's time; in common usage, the anniversary of a person's death.*

yarmulke. *A skullcap worn as a sign of respect to God.*

Yom Kippur. *The Day of Atonement, a day of fasting and prayer; the holiest day in the Jewish calendar.*

City of Memphis
and
Shelby County, Tennessee

Dr. W. W. Herenton
City of Memphis Mayor

A C Wharton, Jr.
Shelby County Mayor

Joint Proclamation

WHEREAS, Temple Israel Congregation was founded in 1854 as B'nai Israel Congregation Children of Israel, and four years later opened its first house of worship at Main and Exchange with great celebration, when Isaac Mayer Wise, the founder of the American Reform Jewish Movement, came here to dedicate the new Temple; and

WHEREAS, Rabbi Jacob J. Peres led the congregation as its first rabbi and served the entire Memphis community as a civic leader, setting a standard of spiritual and community leadership that Temple Israel's ensuing seven rabbis have followed; and

WHEREAS, During the past 150 years, Temple Israel has served as a beacon of hope for this community, dedicated to improving the quality of life for all citizens and sharing religious and social action programs with numerous agencies and organizations; and

WHEREAS, The congregants of Temple Israel historically have given selflessly of themselves to improve the lives of people in this community, from delivering meals to the hungry, giving shelter to the homeless, comforting the sick, and befriending those in need; and

WHEREAS, It is appropriate for Memphis and Shelby County Governments to join all citizens of this great community to offer a prayer of thanks for Temple Israel, which has for 150 years served as an inspiration and role model for all citizens.

NOW, THEREFORE, WE, A C Wharton, Jr., Mayor of Shelby County, Tennessee, and Dr. Willie W. Herenton, Mayor of the City of Memphis, do hereby proclaim Friday, January 16, 2004 to be:

Temple Israel Day

in Memphis and Shelby County and urge all citizens to recognize the contributions and dedication of Temple Israel to our community and let us say, *Yasher Koach*, may your strength increase.

In witness whereof, I have hereunto set my hand and caused the seal of Shelby County to be affixed this 16th day of January 2004.

A C Wharton, Jr.
Mayor of Shelby County

In witness whereof, I have hereunto set my hand and caused the seal of the City of Memphis to be affixed this 16th day of January 2004.

Willie W. Herenton
Mayor of Memphis

United States House of Representatives

PROCLAMATION
by
Congressman Harold Ford
Congresswoman Marsha Blackburn

WHEREAS, Temple Israel was founded in Memphis on March 2, 1854;

WHEREAS, Temple Israel celebrates its 150th Anniversary with a community-wide celebration and Shabbat service entitled "The Dynamism of the Present" on the evening of January 16, 2004;

WHEREAS, with 1,850 member families, Temple Israel is the largest and oldest synagogue in Memphis, and the 13th largest Reform Jewish congregation in North America;

WHEREAS, Temple Israel has enriched the social fabric and spiritual life of Memphis through 150 years of partnerships and service;

WHEREAS, the Temple Israel congregation, through activism and service to the broader community, has embodied the Jewish tradition of tikkun olam, repairing the world;

WHEREAS, under the leadership of Rabbi James A. Wax, of Blessed Memory, Temple Israel's congregants stood alongside Memphians of all colors and faiths to advance social justice and racial harmony during the Civil Rights Movement;

WHEREAS, as Chairman of the Memphis Inter-Faith Alliance, Rabbi Emeritus Harry Danziger has carried forward Temple Israel's rich tradition of service to the greater Memphis community;

WHEREAS, Temple Israel and its congregants have supported the work of more than 60 religious, educational, and social action organizations in the Memphis community, delivering meals to the hungry, providing shelter to the homeless, comforting the sick and befriending those in need;

WHEREAS, as President of the Memphis Ministers Association, Rabbi Micah Greenstein plays a critical role in building greater understanding and partnership among Memphis's many faith communities;

WHEREAS, Memphis's tradition of inter-faith partnership serves as a model for communities throughout America;

WHEREAS, devotion to faith, and greater understanding between faiths, are needed to overcome the challenges faced by the Memphis community, the United States, and the world;

WHEREAS, leaders of many faith communities join Temple Israel in celebrating its 150th Anniversary;

It is with great joy that we salute Temple Israel on its 150th Anniversary, wishing peace and good will for the Temple, its congregants, and its many friends of all faiths throughout the Memphis community.

NOW, BE IT THEREFORE RESOLVED, that we, **HAROLD FORD** and **MARSHA BLACKBURN**, Members of Congress, join with the Temple Israel congregation as we celebrate on this 16th day of January, 2004, having set our hands and caused the great seal of the Congress of the United States to become affixed here in Washington, D.C.

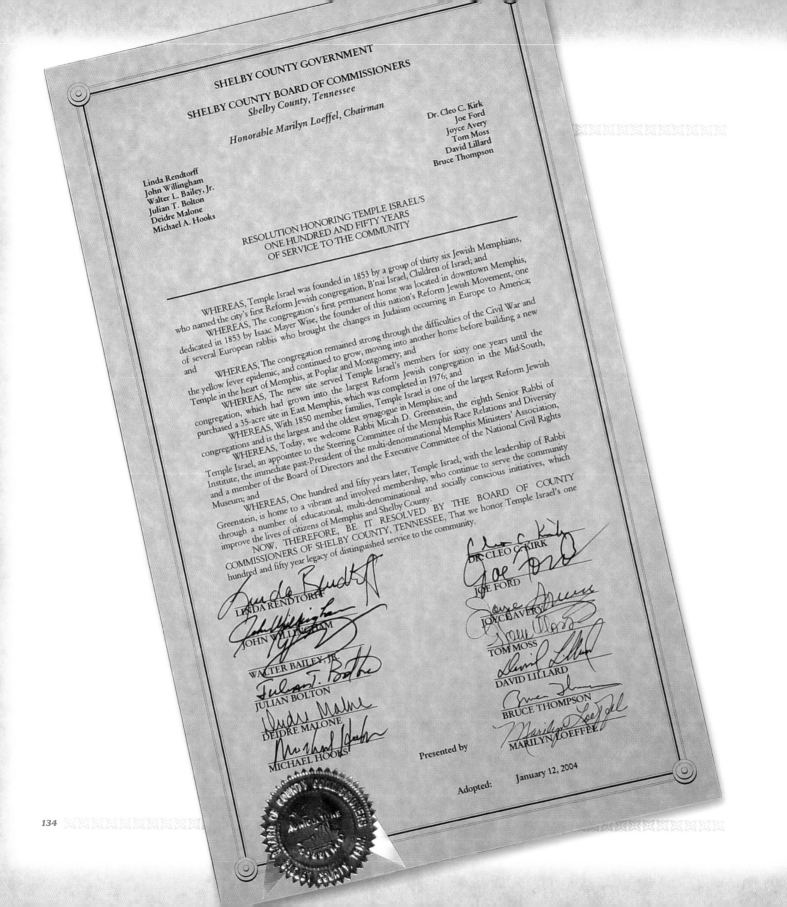

SHELBY COUNTY GOVERNMENT

SHELBY COUNTY BOARD OF COMMISSIONERS
Shelby County, Tennessee

Honorable Marilyn Loeffel, Chairman

Dr. Cleo C. Kirk
Joe Ford
Joyce Avery
Tom Moss
David Lillard
Bruce Thompson

Linda Rendtorff
John Willingham
Walter L. Bailey, Jr.
Julian T. Bolton
Deidre Malone
Michael A. Hooks

RESOLUTION HONORING TEMPLE ISRAEL'S
ONE HUNDRED AND FIFTY YEARS
OF SERVICE TO THE COMMUNITY

WHEREAS, Temple Israel was founded in 1853 by a group of thirty six Jewish Memphians, who named the city's first Reform Jewish congregation, B'nai Israel, Children of Israel; and

WHEREAS, The congregation's first permanent home was located in downtown Memphis, dedicated in 1853 by Isaac Mayer Wise, the founder of this nation's Reform Jewish Movement, one of several European rabbis who brought the changes in Judaism occurring in Europe to America; and

WHEREAS, The congregation remained strong through the difficulties of the Civil War and the yellow fever epidemic, and continued to grow, moving into another home before building a new Temple in the heart of Memphis, at Poplar and Montgomery; and

WHEREAS, The new site served Temple Israel's members for sixty one years until the congregation, which had grown into the largest Reform Jewish congregation in the Mid-South, purchased a 35-acre site in East Memphis, which was completed in 1976; and

WHEREAS, With 1850 member families, Temple Israel is one of the largest Reform Jewish congregations and is the largest and the oldest synagogue in Memphis; and

WHEREAS, Today, we welcome Rabbi Micah D. Greenstein, the eighth Senior Rabbi of Temple Israel, an appointee to the Steering Committee of the Memphis Race Relations and Diversity Institute, the immediate past-President of the multi-denominational Memphis Ministers' Association, and a member of the Board of Directors and the Executive Committee of the National Civil Rights Museum; and

WHEREAS, One hundred and fifty years later, Temple Israel, with the leadership of Rabbi Greenstein, is home to a vibrant and involved membership, who continue to serve the community through a number of educational, multi-denominational and socially conscious initiatives, which improve the lives of citizens of Memphis and Shelby County.

NOW, THEREFORE, BE IT RESOLVED BY THE BOARD OF COUNTY COMMISSIONERS OF SHELBY COUNTY, TENNESSEE, That we honor Temple Israel's one hundred and fifty year legacy of distinguished service to the community.

LINDA RENDTORFF

JOHN WILLINGHAM

WALTER BAILEY, JR.

JULIAN BOLTON

DEIDRE MALONE

MICHAEL HOOKS

DR. CLEO C. KIRK

JOE FORD

JOYCE AVERY

TOM MOSS

DAVID LILLARD

BRUCE THOMPSON

MARILYN LOEFFEL

Presented by

Adopted: January 12, 2004

The State of Tennessee

State Capitol

By Phil Bredesen, Governor, on behalf of the people of Tennessee
By virtue of the authority vested in me, I herby confer upon

Temple Israel

A Day of Recognition

Given under my hand and the Seal of the State of Tennessee
in Nashville, this 16th day of January, 2004

Phil Bredesen
Governor

Source Notes

CHAPTER ONE

1 *Daily Appeal,* 16 September 1858.
2 John E. Harkins, *Metropolis of the American Nile: An Illustrated History of Memphis and Shelby County* (Oxford, Mississippi: The Guild Bindery Press, 1982), 67.
3 Ibid., 51.
4 Paul Flowers, "Paul Flowers' Greenhouse," *The Commercial Appeal,* 7 May 1957.
5 Selma S. Lewis, *A Biblical People in the Bible Belt: The Jewish Community of Memphis, Tennessee, 1840s-1960s* (Macon, Georgia: Mercer University Press, 1998), 2.
6 Harkins, *Metropolis,* 62.
7 Lewis, *A Biblical People,* 7-8.
8 Malcolm H. Stern, *Americans of Jewish Descent: A Compendium of Genealogy* (Cincinnati: Hebrew Union College Press, 1960), 10 and 185.
9 Lewis, *A Biblical People,* 8.; Perre Magness, "Jews Came to Memphis in the 1840's," *The Commercial Appeal,* 7 April 1988.
10 Lewis, *A Biblical People,* 8.
11 Italics added.
12 Lewis, *A Biblical People,* 10.
13 The Children of Israel v. Peres, 42 *Tennessee,* 620, quoted in Lewis, *A Biblical People,* 10, and James A. Wax, "The Jews of Memphis: 1860-1865," West Tennessee Historical Society Papers, No. 3 (1949), 4.

CHAPTER TWO

14 Helen G. and James A. Wax, *Our First Century: 1854-1954* (Memphis: Temple Israel, 1954), 18.
15 Ibid., 18-19.
16 Harkins, *Metropolis,* 72.
17 Lewis, *A Biblical People,* 32;
18 Lewis, *A Biblical People,* 33.
19 Jacob Rader Marcus, *United States Jewry, 1776-1985, Vol. III* (Detroit: Wayne State University Press, 1993), 31-32.
20 A. E. Frankland, "The American Jew's Annual," Temple Israel Archives, 93.
21 Jacob C. Cohen to *The Jewish Messenger,* 2 June 1863, available from www. Jewish-history.com/jcc06.html
22 Ibid.
23 James A. Wax, "The Jews of Memphis: 1860-1865," West Tennessee Historical Society Papers, No. 3 (1949), 20-25.
24 Ibid., 27.

25 Bertram Wallace Korn, *American Jewry and the Civil War* (Philadelphia: The Jewish Publication Society of America, 1957), 122.
26 Ibid.
27 Ibid., 125.
28 Ibid., 122-126.
29 Cohen to *The Jewish Messenger,* 6 May 1863.
30 Korn, *American Jewry,* 154.
31 Ibid., 135.
32 Ibid.

CHAPTER THREE

33 Wax and Wax, *Our First Century,* 22.
34 Harkins, *Metropolis,* 88.
35 Ibid.
36 Ibid.
37 Ibid., 91.
38 A.E. Frankland, *Report on the Yellow Fever Epidemic in Memphis, Tenn.,* 1873 (Memphis: Price, Jones and Co., 1873), 13-14.
39 Ibid.
40 Ibid., 9.
41 Lewis, *A Biblical People,* 59-60.
42 Wax and Wax, *Our First Century,* 25 and 31.

CHAPTER FOUR

43 Harkins, *Metropolis,* 96.
44 Robert A. Sigafoos, *Cotton Row to Beale Street: A Business History of Memphis* (Memphis: Memphis State University Press, 1979), 97.
45 Harkins, *Metropolis,* 98.
46 Ibid., 99-101.
47 Ibid., 102.
48 Ibid.
49 Ibid., 108.
50 Ibid., 113.
51 Sam Shankman, *Baron Hirsch Congregation: From Ur to Memphis* (Memphis: Baron Hirsch Synagogue, 1957), 41; Lewis, *A Biblical People,* 77-78; *Inventory of the Church and Synagogue Archives of Tennessee: Jewish Congregations* (Nashville: The Historical Records Survey, 1941), 29.

[52] Lewis, *A Biblical People,* 77; *The Jewish Spectator*, March 1897, as quoted in Shankman, *Baron Hirsch,* 43.

[53] Ibid., 61-62.

[54] Babette M. Becker, "Chronicle of the Congregation," (Memphis: Temple Israel, 1929), 19. (Temple Israel Archives).

CHAPTER FIVE

[55] Ibid., 22.

[56] Wax and Wax, *Our First Century,* 36; *The Jewish Spectator* (Memphis and New Orleans), 9 October, 1915.

CHAPTER SIX

[57] *The Commercial Appeal,* 19 January 1912.

[58] Ibid., 12 May 1912.

[59] Harry W. Ettelson to the Rev. Robert Jones, 11 June 1942, Ettelson Papers, Temple Israel Archives.

[60] Becker, "Chronicle," 26.

[61] Wax and Wax, *Our First Century,* 39.

[62] Ibid., 41.

[63] Berkley Kalin, "Rabbi William H. Fineshriber: The Memphis Years," in The West Tennessee Historical Society Papers, No. 25 (Memphis: The West Tennessee Historical Society, 1971), 48; Perre Magness, "Memphis Once Suffragism Hotbed," *The Commercial Appeal,* 16 August 1990.

[64] Kalin, "Fineshriber," 47.

[65] "Blue Laws Damnable," an undated clipping from *The Commercial Appeal* included in the Fineshriber folder, Mississippi Valley Archives Collection, as quoted in Kalin, "Fineshriber," 61.

[66] *The Commercial Appeal,* 23 and 25 March 1922 and the Memphis *Press,* 25 March 1922, as cited in Kalin, "Fineshriber," 54.

[67] Kalin, "Fineshriber," 54.

[68] Ibid., 51.

[69] "Mob Action Condemned," *The Commercial Appeal,* 23 May 1917, p. 8; The Commercial Appeal, 25 May 1917.

[70] "Fineshriber Will Preach on Ku Klux Klan Tonight," *The Commercial Appeal,* 14 October 1921, p. 10.

[71] "Fineshriber Assails 'Mob Law' of K.K.K.," *The Commercial Appeal,* 15 October 1921, p. 10; Kalin, "Fineshriber," 52.

[72] Kalin, "Fineshriber," 53.

[73] Ibid., 52-53.

[74] *(Memphis) News-Scimitar,* 30 March 1924, as quoted in Kalin, "Fineshriber," 61-62.

CHAPTER SEVEN

[75] Harry W. Ettelson, "Inaugural Sermon" (delivered at Temple Israel, Memphis, Tenn., 3 April 1925), Ettelson Papers, Temple Israel Archives.

[76] Wax and Wax, *Our First Century,* 44.

CHAPTER EIGHT

[77] Wax and Wax, *Our First Century,* 52.

[78] Michael A. Meyer and W. Gunther Plaut, "Zionism and Israel," in *The Reform Judaism Reader: North American Documents* (New York: UAHC Press, 2000), 133.

[79] Ibid., 139.

[80] Simon Wener, president, Memphis Zionist District, to Temple Israel, 20 November 1948, Ettelson Papers, Temple Israel Archives.

[81] Mortimer May to Harry W. Ettelson, 3 June 1943, Ettelson Papers, Temple Israel Archives.

[82] Harry W. Ettelson to Mortimer May, 22 June 1943, Ettelson Papers, Temple Israel Archives.

[83] Harry W. Ettelson to Arthur J. Lelyveld, 12 April 1945, Ettelson Papers, Temple Israel Archives.

CHAPTER NINE

[84] James A. Wax, "The One Hope" (sermon delivered at Temple Israel, Memphis, TN, 25 September 1946), Wax Papers, Temple Israel Archives.

[85] Joan Beifuss, "Profile: Rabbi James Wax," *Memphis* magazine (February 1981), 41.

[86] Lewis, *A Biblical People,* 193-198.

[87] Jocelyn Rudner, interview by author, Memphis, Tenn., 31 March 2003.

[88] Patricia M. LaPointe, "The Prophetic Voice: Rabbi James A. Wax," in *The Quiet Voices: Southern Rabbis and Black Civil Rights, 1880s to 1990s,* ed. Mark K. Bauman and Berkley Kalin (Tuscaloosa: University of Alabama Press, 1997), 163.

[89] Ibid., 153;

Source Notes

90 James A. Wax, "Dr. Martin Luther King, Jr." (sermon delivered at Temple Israel, Memphis, TN, 5 April 1968), Rabbi James A. Wax Collection, Memphis-Shelby County Public Library and Information Center.

91 Henry Loeb to James Wax, 18 June 1971, Wax Papers, Temple Israel Archives.

92 Tom Bailey, Jr., "Friends Recall Legacy of Wax," *The Commercial Appeal,* 19 October 1989, p. B1.

93 Abe Plough to S.L. Kopald, 2 June 1960, Temple Israel Archives.

CHAPTER TEN

94 SoFTY is an acronym for the Southern Federation of Temple Youth.

95 Herschel Feibelman, interview by author, 23 May 2002.

96 Ibid.; Alfred Alperin, telephone conversation with author, Feb. 2004.

CHAPTER ELEVEN

97 Harry K. Danziger, "But Do We Look Jewish? The Trunk in the Attic" (sermon delivered at Temple Israel in Memphis, TN, 27 September 1973), in *Double Chai* (Memphis: Temple Israel, 2000), 49.

98 Bailey, "Friends Recall Legacy," p. B1.

CHAPTER TWELVE

99 "The Assassination," *Time,* 12 April 1968, 18.

CHAPTER THIRTEEN

100 Howard R. Greenstein and Micah D. Greenstein, "Then and Now," in *The Quiet Voices: Southern Rabbis and Black Civil Rights, 1880s to 1990s,* ed. by Mark K. Bauman and Berkley Kalin. (Tuscaloosa: University of Alabama Press, 1998).

101 Micah D. Greenstein, "A Jewish Response to the 9-11 Attacks on America" (sermon delivered at Temple Israel, 17 September 2001).

Bibliography

BOOKS AND ARTICLES

Anshei Sphard-Beth El Emeth Congregation. *Dedication Booklet.* Memphis: Anshei-Sphard-Beth El Emeth Congregation, 13 September 1970.

Bauman, Mark K., and Berkley Kalin, eds. *The Quiet Voices: Southern Rabbis and Black Civil Rights, 1880s to 1990s.* Tuscaloosa: University of Alabama Press, 1997.

Becker, Babette M. "Chronicle of the Congregation." Memphis: Temple Israel, 1929.

Beifuss, Joan Turner. *At the River I Stand: Memphis, the 1968 Strike, and Martin Luther King.* Memphis: B and W Books, 1985.

Beifuss, Joan Turner. "Profile: Rabbi James Wax." *Memphis,* February 1981.

Capers, Gerald M., Jr. *Biography of a Rivertown.* New Orleans: Tulane University Press, 1966.

Cohen, Jacob C. "Letters to *The Jewish Messenger,*" 6 May-2 June 1863. Available from www.Jewish-history.com/jcc06.html.

Danziger, Harry K. *Double Chai: A Collection of Writings on the Occasion of His Retirement.* Memphis: Temple Israel, 2000.

Ettelson, Harry W. Papers. Temple Israel Archives.

Evans, Eli N. *The Provincials: A Personal History of Jews in the South.* New York: Atheneum, 1973.

Fineshriber, William H. Papers. Temple Israel Archives.

Frankland, A.E. "The American Jew's Annual." N.p., n.d. (Temple Israel Archives)

Frankland, A.E. *Report on the Yellow Fever Epidemic in Memphis, Tenn., 1873.* Memphis: Price, Jones and Co., 1873.

Hall, Jay. "A Man for All People." *The Commercial Appeal,* 26 February 1978.

Harkins, John E. *Metropolis of the American Nile: Memphis and Shelby County.* Oxford, Mississippi: The Guild Bindery Press, in cooperation with the West Tennessee Historical Society, Inc., 1982.

Inventory of the Church and Synagogue Archives of Tennessee: Jewish Congregations. Nashville: The Historical Records Survey, 1941.

Kalin, Berkley. "Rabbi William H. Fineshriber: The Memphis Years." In *The West Tennessee Historical Society Papers, no. 25.* Memphis: The West Tennessee Historical Society, 1971.

Korn, Bertram Wallace. *American Jewry and the Civil War.* Philadelphia: The Jewish Publication Society of America, 1957.

Lewis, Selma S. *A Biblical People in the Bible Belt: The Jewish Community of Memphis, Tennessee, 1840s-1960s.* Macon, Georgia: Mercer University Press, 1998.

Lewis, Selma S., and Norman Shapiro. "The Rabbis of Temple Israel." Unpublished manuscript.

Malamut, Joseph L., and Milton W. Goldberger, eds. *Southern Jewry: An Account of Jewish Progress and Achievement in the Southland.* Memphis: *The Hebrew Watchman,* 1933.

Marcus, Jacob Rader. *United States Jewry, 1776-1985, vols. 2 and 3.* Detroit: Wayne State University Press, 1993.

Meyer, Michael A., and W. Gunther Plaut. "Zionism and Israel." In *The Reform Judaism Reader: North American Documents.* New York: UAHC Press, 2000.

Sachar, Howard M. *A History of the Jews in America.* New York: Alfred A. Knopf, 1992.

Samfield, Max Papers. Temple Israel Archives.

Shankman, Sam. *Baron Hirsch Congregation: From Ur to Memphis.* Memphis: Baron Hirsch Synagogue, 1957.

Bibliography

Sigafoos, Robert A. *Cotton Row to Beale Street: A Business History of Memphis.* Memphis: Memphis State University Press, 1979.

Stern, Malcolm H. *Americans of Jewish Descent: A Compendium of Genealogy.* Cincinnati: Hebrew Union College Press, 1960.

Temple Israel. *Minutes of the Congregation,* 1857-2004.

Wax, James A. "The Jews of Memphis: 1860-1865." In *The West Tennessee Historical Society Papers, no. 3.* Memphis: West Tennessee Historical Society, 1949.

Wax, James A. Papers. Temple Israel Archives.

Wax, James A., and Helen G. Wax. *Our First Century: 1854-1954.* Memphis: Temple Israel, 1954.

Wax, Rabbi James A. Collection. Memphis/Shelby County Public Library and Information Center.

PERIODICALS

(Memphis) Commercial Appeal

(Memphis) Daily Appeal

(Temple Israel) Duffel Bag

(Memphis) Hebrew Watchman

Jewish Spectator

Memphis magazine, February 1981.

Memphis Press-Scimitar

Papyrus (a publication of Children of Israel's Junior Congregation)

(Temple Israel) Voice

Time magazine, 12 April 1968

INTERVIEWS

Unless otherwise indicated, all interviews were conducted by the author in Memphis, Tennessee.

Bearman, Leo Jr., 3 October 2002.

Cooper, Frankie, 19 December 2002.

Danziger, Rabbi Harry, 22 October 2002.

Feibelman, Herschel, 23 May 2002.

Golden, Rabbi Constance, by telephone, 9 October 2002.

Greenstein, Rabbi Micah, 26 June 2003.

Kaplan, Cantor John, 27 June 2003.

Kopald, S.L. Jr., 16 July 2002.

Lewis, H. Kirke, 5 May 2003.

Mansberg, Barbara, 12 June 2003.

Ringel, Neil (Nick), 12 April 2003.

Royal, Judith, May 2003

Rudner, Jocelyn, 31 March 2003.

Scheidt, Rudi Sr., October 2003.

Schwartz, Mildred, 8 October 2002.

Wax, Helen, 29 July 2002.

Wurzburg, Kenneth, December 2003.